Computing for College Writing

Revised Twelfth Edition

Department of Composition
University of Minnesota - Duluth

William A. Gibson, Kenneth Risdon, Diana Risdon, and Composition Staff

Pearson
Custom
Publishing

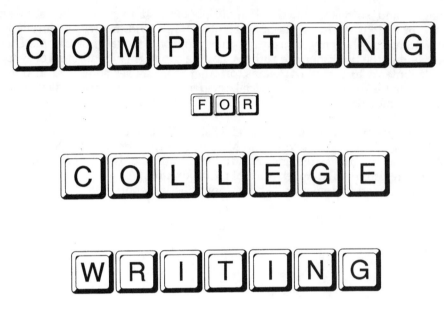

COMPUTING FOR COLLEGE WRITING

Twelfth Edition
REVISED

Diana Risdon

Kenneth Risdon

William A. Gibson

Department of Composition

University of Minnesota, Duluth

WordPerfect is a registered trademark of Corel Systems Corporation.
IBM is a trademark of International Business Machines Corporation.
MS-DOS, Word, and Windows are registered trademarks of Microsoft Corporation.
FrameMaker is a registered trademark of Adobe Corporation.
Macintosh is a registered trademark of Apple Computer, Incorporated.

Printed in the United States of America

10 9 8 7 6 5 4 3 2

This manuscript was supplied camera-ready by the author.

Please visit our web site at www.pearsoncustom.com

ISBN 0–536–66807–8

BA 996162

PEARSON CUSTOM PUBLISHING
75 Arlington Street, Suite 300, Boston, MA 02116
A Pearson Education Company

Composition 1120 Lab Policies

Course Materials

For the COMP 1120 computing component, each student must purchase a course manual and disks:

Risdon, Diana, et. al. *Computing for College Writing*. Minneapolis: Pearson, 2001.

At least two 3.5 inch, DSHD (double-sided, high density) floppy disks.

At the end of the quarter, you will be asked to turn in a disk containing all of the files that you completed in COMP 1120, College Writing.

Attendance

Attendance at **all** class sessions is **mandatory**. You can more easily complete computing lessons during the assigned class period than on your own. Help may not always be available outside of class. AVOID FRUSTRATION: ATTEND CLASS. If it is necessary for you to miss more than one or two class sessions, you may be asked to drop the course and take it at another time. Arrange your schedule so that you can come to class ON TIME. If you are late, you will have to catch up on your own. Don't expect the class to stop and wait for you. If you do drop the class, it is your responsibility to process the proper forms through the Registrar's Office.

Assignments

Expect to complete weekly exercises and out-of-class assignments, including review worksheets. The College Writing final examination will be done in the a computer laboratory at a scheduled time. Doing the assignments in the assigned sequence is important. All assignments and exercises must be completed and turned in on time to pass the course. Late assignments will result in lower grades.

Disabilities

Individuals having any permanent or temporary disability which might affect their performance in this class are encouraged to inform the instructor at the start of the session. Methods, materials, or testing can be adapted as required to ensure equitable participation.

Lesson 1 — Getting Started

The process of learning to write is a complex one. Computer use and word processing are so important as tools for writers that we require all students in college writing to know how to write and revise on a computer. Word processing is valuable because once you know how to operate the system, you will be able to devote the majority of your time to the more important matters of writing well: learning the writing process, logic, organization, stylistic choices, and revision. Word processing should change the proportion of time you spend in doing different writing tasks:

- Correcting grammatical and typographical errors becomes easier because the computer does all the reformatting for you. In addition, many spelling, style, and grammar checkers are available to help you in writing and revising your work.

- Making major revisions in your work becomes simpler because the word processor enables you to combine paragraphs, rearrange sentences or paragraphs, or add and delete text. With it you can focus on the structure and content of the essay. You learn how to write well by devoting your time to writing and revising, not by spending time mechanically typing revisions.

- Rather than writing out your essays long hand and then typing them, you can develop the skill of composing at the computer, thus eliminating one step in the composing process.

Word processing is a practical skill that will help you in college writing and other courses as you learn more about the logic and structure of academic writing. It is also the beginning of computer literacy. Once you understand the logic and structure of a computer and a word processing program, you can easily go on to learn how to use other useful computer tools such as desktop publishing, graphics programs, information retrieval, and electronic mail.

We have emphasized word processing in college writing because it will be beneficial to you in three different situations:

Learning to write well: Word processing will allow you to write more efficiently, equipping you with a tool that will serve you well through college writing, advanced writing, and any other writing assignments at the university level and beyond.

Communicating with your instructors: When your instructors receive word processed papers, they not only will be able to read your writing more easily, but they also will be better able to make suggestions for improvement. The revising process will be easier for both student and instructor with the assistance of a word processor. Your college writing instructor may ask you to turn in your written work on a disk as well as in print form.

Working in the community beyond the University: Not only can word processing prove valuable in an academic setting, but it also is a widely marketable skill. Businesses, industries, human service organizations, and government agencies depend increasingly on computers. Many employers today expect job candidates at all levels from clerical to managerial and administrative to know the basics of computer use, especially word processing. In an age increasingly dominated by the use of information, many employees will not only write in their jobs; they will also edit, lay out, and publish information for company and public consumption. Thus knowledge of writing and computers has become a necessity, not an option.

Why Windows 2000

Every computer system uses an operating system that controls how the computer works internally and how the user interacts with the computer to perform various tasks. Although there are numerous operating systems, for example, DOS, Unix, System 7, OS/2, Windows 3.x, we will be using Microsoft's Windows 2000 (Win2000). Win2000 is built around a Graphic User Interface (GUI), the term for how the computer screen looks to a user, which is similar throughout all the programs that run in the Win2000 environment. Although a new user of Win2000 will have to learn new terminology, once you know that terminology, it will apply to any Win2000 programs you learn in the future.

Similarly, a variety of word processing programs exist. Each one has somewhat different features and operates in slightly different ways. Two of the more popular programs are Microsoft Word 2000 and Corel WordPerfect 2000. We will feature both programs throughout this course and refer only to a generic word processing program as WP. Once you know the basics in one program, you can quite easily adjust to another program.

Equipment Overview

A computer consists of the following components (hardware) that interact with each other as a unit:

- The **Central Processing Unit** (CPU) is the core of the computer. It coordinates the computer activities and allows it to perform logical and arithmetic functions.

- **Computer Memory** consists of a series of specialized microchips necessary for CPU function. The two types are ROM and RAM:

  Read Only Memory (ROM) is fixed memory that is used to store programs and instructions the computer uses often. The data in ROM cannot be changed and is not affected either by turning the computer off or by power failure.

  Random Access Memory (RAM) is the part of memory you use as you work with WP or any other program. Unlike ROM, RAM is temporary storage. Its contents, some of

which appear on the screen, will be lost
should the computer be turned off or the
power source fail.

- The **Disk Drives** are used to supply information
to the computer and to store information.
The disk drives most commonly
used have magnetic storage media, similar
to that used on video tape. The drives are of
four basic types: hard disk drives, floppy
disk drives, Zip disk drives, and CD-ROM/
DVD disk drives.

  Hard disk drives (also called fixed disks)
  are usually installed inside the CPU case.
  They have a magnetic coating on multiple
  aluminum platters turning constantly at high
  speed while the computer is in operation.
  They permit both the storage of a great deal
  of information and the transfer of it quickly.
  Computers with hard disks usually load and
  run programs (such as WP) directly from the
  hard disk, usually called Drive C. All of the
  computers in labs on campus are also connected to a series of network hard drives
  located in other buildings and other computers. Most computers equipped with hard
  drives also have one or more floppy disk
  drives as well, usually called Drive A or Drive
  B, which enable users to preserve copies of
  their work on floppy disks.

- **Floppy disk drives**, which are accessible
from the front of the computer, are usually 3
¾".

The 3 ¾" double-sided high-density (DSHD) disks can store about 1.4 million bytes (1.4 MB). DSHD disks are usually marked with the letters HD; they have a small rectangular hole opposite the hole with a sliding tab. Warning: If you format any floppy disk, all your information will be destroyed.

- **Zip™ disk drives**, (usually Drive D or E) located on the front of the computer, accept large capacity storage disks. These disks are similar to floppy disks, except that they usually hold 100 to 250 million bytes (100 to 250 MB). With the increasing size of documents that contain graphics and tables, it may be necessary to save the document to a zip disk because it is too large to put on a regular floppy disk. Zip disks also allow you to back up all your work on one disk.

- **CD-ROM/DVD disk drives** (usually Drive D or E) are similar to your music or video disks. The difference is that the computerís CD-ROM/DVD disk drives can access both data and, if the computer has a sound card and video card, play music and video from the disk. With a CD-ROM disk, you can also write to the CD-ROM disk. Many software programs including WP now come on CD-ROM because the CD-ROM holds up to 650 million bytes (650 MB); loading software is much easier when you don't have to insert numerous 3.5" floppy disks.

- The **Keyboard** is similar to that of a typewriter, with the addition of several special keys which will be explained as you begin to use them.

- The **Monitor** looks like a television screen which displays the document you are working on. Information displayed on the screen exists only in RAM and will be lost if you turn off the computer without first saving your work.

- The **Mouse** is a device with two or three buttons and often a wheel that allows you to control the computer without using the keyboard. It may be set for right- (default) or left-handed use.

- The **Printer** is a device that allows you to transfer data from the screen or disk drives to paper. The on-screen version of your work is called a soft copy; the printed version is referred to as a hard copy.

- A **Network** is a system of hardware and software that allows you to communicate with other computers around campus or throughout the world. For the most part, the only time you will notice that your computer is networked is when you see a file directory with many drives lettered for example F through Z.

Software

All the components described above make up the computer's hardware. However, the hardware is relatively useless without extremely detailed instructions. These sets of instructions, called software or programs, allow a computer to perform different tasks such as word processing, desktop publishing, manipulating graphics, and communicating with other computers.

Most of the software you use is stored either on the hard drive — usually designated as C:\ — or on a network drive. You will use either 3 ¾" floppy disks or zip disks to store the documents you create. You must handle the disks, including CD-ROM discs, with care to insure safekeeping of your work and programs or music. Here are some guidelines to follow when handling disks:

1. Do not allow disks to come in contact with anything that will crease them or scratch their exposed surfaces.

2. Avoid touching the exposed surface of the disk. Oil from your fingers will usually render the disk unreadable and unusable.

3. Remove disks from or insert them into the drives only when the light in front of the drive is off. When the light is on, the computer is either reading from or writing to the disk. Attempting to insert or remove disks at this time could damage both the disk and the drive mechanism. The light is usually on for only a few seconds at a time.

4. Keep the disks from extremes in temperature. Disks can survive -50 to +125 degrees Fahrenheit, but either extreme can cause lost memory or reduced sensitivity.

This may seem like a lot to remember, but a little common sense in handling disks will keep things running smoothly. But because accidents do happen and occasionally a disk will go bad, get in the habit of making duplicate (backup) copies of your work on one or more separate disks.

Files

When using computers, the documents you create or revise are referred to as files. Think of the disk as a drawer in a filing cabinet; within that drawer are file folders that contain information. To access the information in one of these files, you would first open the drawer and select the needed file folder. Next, you would open the file folder and proceed to add, delete, or change information in the individual file. When finished, you would close the folder and return it to the drawer.

The disk is like an electronic file drawer. It contains individual folders from which you can select a particular file to revise on screen. Opening the electronic file folder to access the information requires loading the file into memory. After you have completed the revisions, you close the file and return it to the electronic drawer. You can also add new files (or folders) to or delete files (or folders) from the electronic drawer.

Although the filing cabinet analogy is appropriate, you will find that when working on the computer you will need to do more than go to a filing cabinet and pull open one of its four drawers. The computer's operating system is set up so that there can be hundreds of filing cabinets, each with dozens of drawers with hundreds of folders and files. Because of this, you will need to be able to tell the computer exactly where you filed your document. That is, you need to tell it the exact path leading to the file. This path includes not only the drive (usually designated as A:\, B:\, C:\, etc.) but also the folder (directory or subdirectory) and filename.

The Keyboard

The computer keyboard is similar to that of a typewriter with several additional keys. Click each of the keys below to learn more about the keys.

- **Function Keys** — FI Many keyboards have keys labeled F1 through F12, usually across the top. These are the special function keys which can be used in WP and other software programs. They have been set up by software manufacturers to save keystrokes (and therefore time) when using the programs. For example, in some programs F1 brings up Help, in other programs F3 performs this function. Because software manufacturers assign functions to these keys and because you can assign functions to any of the keys, we will concentrate more on using the toolbars and mouse rather than function keys.

  The function keys can work alone or in combination with the Ctrl, Shift, and Alt command keys. When using command keys, you must first press the appropriate command key or keys (Ctrl, Shift, and/or Alt), hold it down, and then firmly but quickly press the appropriate F1 - F12 function key.

- **Command Keys** — Several other keys surrounding the alphabetic keyboard are called command keys. They are designed to help you do tasks beyond just entering text.

The **Shift** keys are similar to the shift keys on a typewriter. When you press Shift together with a character, it allows you to capitalize that letter and it allows you to type the characters and figures above the numbers or punctuation marks. It also is used in combinations with other keys to perform specific functions such as Shift-Tab releases the margin or Shift-Insert performs a paste.

The **Ctrl** and **Alt** keys too are used in combination with the function keys or in conjunction with other keys. The Ctrl key performs many of the functions that are standard across many Windows software programs: Ctrl-u underlines text, Ctrl-b bolds text, Ctrl-x cuts, Ctrl-v pastes, Ctrl c-copies, Ctrl-s saves, and Ctrl-o opens.

The **Tab** key is similar to the tab key on a typewriter; it allows you to indent the first line of a paragraph. Most WP have preset or default tabs every ¾" across the line; they are easily reset.

The **Enter** key is used to indicate the end of paragraphs or to leave blank lines in a text.

On a typewriter, you would press the return key at the end of each line. However, you don't need to press Enter at the end of each line since WP automatically determines the line length for you. This process is known as word wrap.

The **Backspace** key (at the upper right of the alphabetic keyboard) is used to erase character(s) to the left of the cursor, the blinking line which indicates your position on the screen.

The **Caps Lock** key is similar to the shift lock key on a typewriter. By pressing it, you can make all letters upper case. It is a toggle key; pressing it once turns capitals on, and pressing it again turns capitals off. Note that Caps Lock affects only the alphabetic keys; the only way to get the special symbols above the numbers at the top of the keyboard or the upper punctuation marks is to use one of the Shift keys.

The **Esc** key exits in some instances or cancels a command in WP.

- **Numeric Keypad** — At the extreme right of the keyboard are keys that resemble the keys on a calculator. They can be used for quickly entering numeric data when the Num Lock key is toggled on and the Num Lock light is lighted. On some keyboards we also use their alternate functions (underneath the numerals), which are available when NumLock is toggled off and the Num Lock light is not lighted. On most keyboards these alternate function keys are located between the alphabetic keyboard and the numeric keypad.

The ten specialized cursor movement keys perform exactly the same, whether you use them on the keypad or off. The keys with directional arrows (under the keypad numbers 2, 4, 6, and 8, respectively) are used for moving the cursor slowly through the text on the screen. The PgUp (under 9), PgDn (under 3), +, -, Home (under 7), and End (under 1) keys provide you with quicker ways to move through longer texts. The 0 Ins key is the Insert/Typeover toggle key. The Del functions as a delete key which erases the character at the cursor position and one character at a time to the right.

An Alternative to the Keyboard

The Graphic User Interface (GUI) of Win2000 can more easily be controlled with the mouse than the function or control keys on the keyboard. Movement of the mouse produces various pointers on the computer screen. The default mouse pointer in text is a white arrow. Do not confuse this pointer with the cursor, which is a straight, blinking, vertical bar. To reposition the cursor using the mouse, move the arrow to the position in the text where you want the cursor and click the left mouse button. Additional uses of the mouse will be explained as various functions are introduced. (For right-handed use, the left mouse button performs the primary mouse functions, so this key may be taken for granted unless otherwise specified.

The left and right mouse buttons may be reversed in their functions for left-handed users).

To use the mouse in Win2000 you need to understand several key terms used throughout this course.

- **Selecting** — To select an item, move the mouse pointer to the item, press the left mouse button once and quickly release it. This action is called clicking the mouse once. You can select menu choices, icons, group icons, or buttons, which are graphic representations of "buttons" like those found on stereos, VCRs, etc. They work much the same way except that you "press" them by clicking the mouse (or pressing Enter) instead of pressing them with your finger. In this manual, select means **one** mouse click.

- **Opening** — To open or start an application, move the mouse pointer to the item or icon, press the left mouse button twice quickly. This action is called double clicking. In this manual, open means **two** mouse clicks.

- **Dragging** — To move an icon, window, or dialog box, move the mouse pointer to the icon or the title bar, press and hold down the left mouse button, and drag it to the desired location by moving the mouse right, left, up, or down on the mouse pad and releasing the mouse button. To highlight text insert the I-bar at the desired location, press and hold down the left mouse button, and drag the highlight through the text by moving the mouse on the mouse pad. When you reach the end of the text to be highlighted, release the mouse button.

- **Sizing** — To size a window move the mouse pointer to the edge of the window. When you are in the right place, the mouse pointer will change to a double headed arrow which shows which direction you can drag the edge. When you have this double headed arrow, press and hold the left mouse button while moving the mouse until you have the desired size and shape, then release the button.

The Win2000 Screen

The background of the Win2000 screen is known as the desktop. On this desktop are various icons which represent shortcuts, or files which point to other files such as software programs, on your computer. To open any of the shortcut programs, double click the icon. An alternative is to display the Start Menu by clicking Start, a button at the left of the taskbar, the bar at the bottom of the screen. Depending on how your computer is set up, you will see various items such as Programs, Documents, Settings, Search, Help, Run, and Shut Down in the Start Menu. To access programs not on the desktop, click Programs and select the program from the list.

Look at the graphic of the Win 2000 screen on the next page and identify the main portions of the desktop: Shortcuts, Start button, Taskbar shortcuts, Active programs, System tray, and Clock.

The Win2000 Desktop

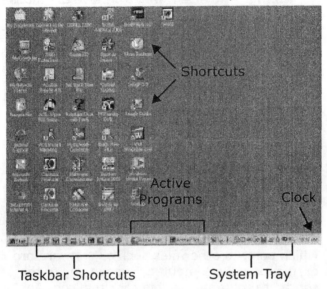

Taskbar Shortcuts   System Tray

- **Shortcuts** — Each of the icons on the desktop represents a program or folders you can access by double clicking the icon. You can add shortcuts to your desktop by creating a shortcut in Windows Explorer and dragging it to your desktop.

- **Start** — Clicking the Start button allows you to control your computer. Most frequently used is the Programs selection from which you can select any of the software programs loaded on your computer. Sometimes you cannot see all the programs listed. If two

carets appear at the bottom of the list, click
them to see more selections. If you see a
triangle to the right of a selection, you will
have to click the selection to see the additional selection choices.

- **Taskbar Shortcuts** — In addition to putting
  shortcuts on your desktop, you can add frequently used software programs to the taskbar, the bar at the bottom of your Win2000
  screen, by dragging a shortcut from your
  desktop or Windows Explorer to the taskbar.
  You can also delete the shortcuts from the
  taskbar by right clicking the mouse over the
  program you want to delete and then selecting Delete.

- **Active Programs** — The taskbar also shows
  an icon for all software programs you have
  open, in this case Internet Explorer, Adobe
  Photoshop, two HTML documents in Dream-
  weaver, and Windows Explorer. You can
  work on a Word document, create a spreadsheet in Excel, and resize a graphic in Photoshop without closing any of the programs.
  When you minimize the program, an icon
  appears on the taskbar to indicate the program is still active. Click the icon on the
  taskbar to make the program active.

- **System Tray** — The taskbar also contains
  the system tray. Some software programs
  add icons to this area of the taskbar so that
  you can access the programs easily. In the
  system tray above, you can see On AC
  Power, Volume, Norton AntiVirus Auto-Pro-
  tect Enabled, Screen Display, GoBack, Scan-

ner Not Responding, Direct CD Wizard, Memory Stick, SB Live, Real Player, Create CD, and Camtasia Recorder. You can control some functions of your computer from the system tray such as increase the volume, scan a disk or file, or change the resolution of the display on your monitor.

- **Clock** — The current time appears at the extreme right of the taskbar. The date and time are set in the Settings, Control Panel submenu of the Start button.

The WP Screen

On the WP screen you should now be able to identify: Title bar, Menu bar, Tool bar, Ruler, Scroll bar, Status bar, Win2000 taskbar, and New document.

The WP Screen

When you have opened WP, you see the WP application screen. This screen looks like most other Win2000 application screens with similar features in the same places.

- **Title Bar** — The WP screen is a full screen window with a Title Bar showing the WP icon, the WP program name and the name of the file that is open in the application window. To the right on the Title Bar are the minimize, resize, and exit buttons.

  ▬┛ allows you to minimize WP and put a button on the Win2000 taskbar.

  🗗 allows you to resize the WP application window so that you can see the Win2000 desktop.

  ☒ allows you to exit WP and return to the Win2000 desktop.

- **Menu Bar** — Below the Title Bar is a Menu Bar with various menu options such as File, Edit, View, Insert, Format, Tools, Table, Window, and Help. Selecting any one of these menu items gives you a drop-down menu with additional menu choices. Click in the right hand corner to close the current document.

- **Tool Bar** — Below the Menu Bar and above the Status Bar you may see a Tool Bar. WP has different Tool Bar sets. Holding the mouse pointer over an individual button gives a Quick Tip that explains what the button does. By pointing the mouse pointer at the Tool Bar and pressing the right mouse button, you can see and change to the other Tool Bar arrangements.

- **Ruler** — A horizontal and vertical Ruler may also appear. The ruler graphically displays the margin settings and the tab settings across the page. To turn the Ruler on or off, click View on the Menu Bar and select Ruler.

- **Scroll Bar** — The extreme right of the screen has a Scroll Bar with an arrow at the top and bottom, and a box somewhere between the arrows to represent graphically the position of the cursor in the current document. There may also be a horizontal Scroll Bar at the bottom of the screen above the Tool Bar and Status Bar. Scrolling does not move the cursor to a new position.

- **Status Bar** — Near the bottom of the screen, you will see the Status Bar. You may see an indicator which tells you whether you are in insert or typeover mode: in insert mode, as you enter text at the cursor location, the existing text moves to the right. If you see Typeover or OVR, you will erase text at the cursor as you enter text. You will also see the page number in the current document, the line position of the cursor in inches from the top margin, and the position of the cursor in inches from the left margin. This message changes depending on where the cursor is located and what you are trying to do.

- **Win2000 Taskbar** — At the bottom of the screen, you will see the familiar Win2000 Taskbar. You can click the Start button, launch a different program, open an active program, and manage your computer from the taskbar.

- **New document** — In the middle of the screen you will see a blank document. The black vertical line is the cursor; when you start typing, your text will appear here at the cursor. You can enter text or open an existing document from this screen.

Format a Disk

To store the word processed papers that you write, you need a disk prepared to receive information from the computer. This requires that a blank, floppy disk be formatted so it is compatible with the computer you are using. If your floppy disk has HD (high density) on it, you will have to format the disk for 1.4 megabytes (MB). Most disks you buy will be aleady formatted. However, you may want to reformat a disk to remove any information on it. Although you can perform this task in various ways, we will use Win2000ís Explorer to do it.

To format a disk, insert the disk in the floppy drive, and click Start, Programs, Accessories, Windows Explorer. Locate the drive where you put the disk, right click on the drive, and select Format. Win2000 automatically detects if a disk is not formatted and gives you an Exploring dialog box asking you if you want to format the disk. Click Yes. Respond to the information in the dialog box. You will see a Formatting progress bar at the bottom of the dialog box showing you the format progress. When Win2000 finishes, you will get a Format Results dialog box showing the results of the format.

⚠ Formatting a disk will erase all the information on a disk. Be sure that the disk you put in the floppy drive does not contain information that you want to keep.

Using Win2000 Explorer

An indispensable tool in Win2000 is Windows Explorer. In addition to using Explorer to format unformatted disks, you will also use it for file management. See the graphic of the Explorer window on the next page.

Notice that the Explorer screen is similar to most Win2000 screens with its Title Bar and minimize, resize, and exit buttons, Menu Bar with various menu options, Toolbar with various buttons, Address indicating the current folder, and Status Bar at the bottom that lists the number of objects, free disk space on the selected drive, and the disk space used on the selected drive.

In the left column you will see a representation of the computer desktop with each drive designated with a letter (A, B, C, D, E, etc.) as a hard drive, floppy drive, CD-ROM, DVD, or Zip drive.

You may have to scroll up or down to see all the drives. Beneath the drives are the folders (directories) that contain other folders and files. To see what a folder contains, click the + to the left of the folder. When there are no more folders to open, you will see a - to the left of the folder. To open a folder, double click the folder. The folders and files contained in this folder appear in the right column.

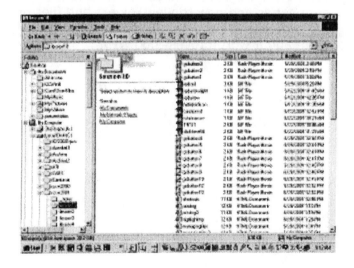

The menu options in Explorer allow you to change the way Explorer displays files and folders. If you select View, Large Icons, you will see icons for folders and files. To display the folders and filenames with file size, type of file, and date modified, select View, Details. You can also change the way the folders and files are listed: select View, Arrange Icons. You can list them by Name (alphabetically by filename), by Type (alphabetically by extension, the last three characters of the filename, dll, exe, ini, for example), by Size (smallest to largest), or by Date (newest to oldest).

A quick way to sort these views in a different way is to click Name, Size, Type, or Modified above the detailed list.

You now know about the computer and its peripherals and how to view folders and files on the computer. In the next lesson you will learn more about word processing (WP).

Lesson 1 - Getting Started Review Questions

Name _____

Section _____

1. What is a GUI?

2. What is the difference between having your WP file in RAM or on a floppy disk?

3. What happens to the information on a floppy disk when you format the disk?

4. What are four basic tasks performed with the mouse?

5. What is a path in computer terminology?

Lesson 1 - Getting Started Review Questions

6. What is the System Tray?

7. How do you minimize a window?

8. What is a Quick Tip?

9. What information does the Status Bar give you?

10. In Windows Explorer what does the View menu allow you to do?

Computing for College Writing

Lesson 2 — Basic Word Processing

To begin a session of word processing, the first step is to load or open your word processing program (referred throughout these lessons as WP). You need to locate the WP shortcut on the desktop, the taskbar shortcut icon, or click Programs, and select the WP program.

This icon is Microsoft Word ; this is Corel WordPerfect .

When you find the WP shortcut on the desktop, double click to open it or click a shortcut icon. When WP is loaded, you will have a blank WP editing window with the cursor in the upper left corner. When you have this empty window, you can begin to type a new document or open an existing one.

Open an Existing Document

Once the cursor is on an empty WP window, you are ready to type in text for a new document or edit a document you have already created. To open an existing document, select Open on the tool bar . The Open dialog box appears. Here you look for the file you want to open. You can tell the current path from the Look in: box .

Look in: My Documents

Notice that Files are listed in the center of the dialog box. To display the details about the files (just like Windows Explorer displays filename, size, type, and modified date), click Views or Details on the tool bar. If the file you want to open is not in the current folder, click the down arrow in the Look in: box to select the correct drive or folder. Again, you may have to scroll up or down to find the right drive. When the correct drive has been selected, double click folders to display their contents. When you have found the file you want, double click to open it, or select it, and click Open.

If you are uncertain which file you want to open, first click Open. Next click Views and select Preview or click Toggle Preview On/Off on the tool bar. A viewer box appears at the right of the screen. Click the file to view it. When you have located the correct file, double click the file to open it.

Navigation

After opening a document, wait for the document to appear on the editing screen. When WP opens a document, it places the cursor in the upper left corner of the first page of the document. Many shortcut methods exist for quickly moving around in a document to locate the position where you want to edit, enter, delete, copy, or move text. In addition to using the arrow buttons and the scroll bar to move around in a document, keys and combination of keys also move the cursor position.

⚠ Using the arrow keys or scroll bar to change location in a document does not move the cursor position. You can tell where the cursor is from the Status Bar. You must click on the text to relocate the cursor on the current page to be able to add new text. If you don't, the text you add will be at the cursor location, possibly many pages away.

Use these key combinations to move through a document:

Arrow keys (left, right, up, and down) move the cursor one character or line at a time in the indicated direction.

Ctrl - right arrow or Ctrl - left arrow moves the cursor to the beginning of the next or previous word.

Home moves the cursor to the left edge of the text column on the same line.

End moves the cursor to the end of the current line.

PgUp moves the cursor to the top of the screen.

PgDn moves the cursor to the bottom of the screen.

Ctrl-Home and Ctrl-End move the cursor to the beginning or end of the document (after most formatting codes).

Ctrl-g gives a Go To dialog box. Type in a page number, and click Go To, OK, or press Enter; WP places the cursor at the top of the page you specified.

Inserting Text

Once you have reached the position you want to edit, you can enter text by typing at the cursor location. Typing in new text causes the existing text to move to the right. Whether you are entering new text in an existing document or creating new text on a blank screen, you do not have to press Enter at the end of each line; WP automatically wraps to the next line when it needs to and reformats the entire paragraph as you continue to type new text. If you press Enter at the end of each line as you type, the text will not reformat properly later when you revise.

WP is preset to insert mode. If you press Ins or Insert, you will be in Typeover mode; in this mode, the text you type is entered over the existing text at the cursor position, erasing the existing text as you continue to type over it. To get out of Typeover mode, simply press Ins or Insert again to return to Insert mode.

Deleting Text

As you enter text, you may need to make corrections. WP can delete information very quickly. To delete a mistake you have just typed, press Backspace to move the cursor one character at a time to the left; as the cursor moves, it erases a single character to its left. If you do not want to erase all the characters between a mistake and the current cursor position, use the arrow keys or mouse to move the cursor to the right of the mistake. Pressing Backspace will erase the mistaken character to its left.

Another way to delete information is to use Del or Delete which erases the character the cursor is on. As you continue to press Del or Delete, each character is erased from the cursor position and to the right. Thus, Backspace erases the character to the left of the cursor while Del erases at the cursor and to the right.

Formatting before Typing Text

WP allows a writer to perform many printing and formatting functions automatically. You will find that performing these functions while word processing becomes automatic with practice. The most common functions for composition purposes are bold, underlining, and italics. Bold, Underline, and Italics require two commands, an on (beginning) and an off (end) to tell the computer which text is to be boldfaced, underlined, or italicized. To perform these functions, you can choose either of two methods: mouse or keystroke.

Using the mouse, select Format, Font or select B, I, or U from the Tool bar. Type the text. When you are finished using bold, underline, or italics, select Format, Font and return to original settings or select B, I, or U from the Tool bar again to turn the function off.

Using keystrokes, press Ctrl-b (Bold), Ctrl-i (Italics), or Ctrl-u (Underline), type the text, and press Ctrl-b, Ctrl-i, or Ctrl-u, to end the function.

Using Center

Unlike Bold, Italics, and Underline, Center requires only one command, although the command may be given and exited several different ways. Selecting the Center button on the Tool bar centers the text you are about to type (or have already typed), as well as all text which may follow. Pressing Enter after the centered text moves the cursor to the center of the next line. To stop centering text, choose a different justification from the Tool bar.

Changing Line Spacing

WP is preset to single space all documents. However, for most of your college papers, you will want to double space your text. Line spacing is a paragraph or line function; look for a Line Spacing button on the tool bar or look in the Format menu.

Creating a Header

Most composition instructors prefer that you use a header to identify each page of your essay. A header is a block of information usually placed in the upper right corner of each page of text by using a special header function. Creating a header with the header function, rather than just typing the information into the body of your document, is much easier because you can create it once, and the computer will automatically place it at the beginning of each page of text.

The header is a Insert or View menu function. Type or edit the header information you want on each page of your document, usually your name, your class and section number, and the assignment number or date in your instructor's prescribed format using any of the function or special keys of WP. The header will be placed at the top of the current page and every page thereafter. Always remember to close your header or click in the document area to avoid typing your document into the header.

You will want to number the pages in your document. To do this, make sure that your cursor is on the page where you want page numbers to begin. Use the Format or Insert menus to add page numbers.

Saving a Document

When you have finished editing a document and wish to quit, you must always SAVE YOUR WORK. If you do not save your work, everything you have done will be gone. If you have not saved your document before, select File, Save, or select the Save button from the Tool bar. You will see the Save File dialog box. Type in a filename for your document, check the Save in: box for the drive and folder path, and press Save. Because computers on occasion do lock up or the power goes off, experienced computer users save their work as they write. Typically, if you pause to think, press the Save button. You can reduce your potential for frustration by saving often.

To name a document, type in a name containing characters, letters, or numbers that identify the document. Win2000 accommodates folder and filenames up to 250 characters long, so you are not limited to the DOS eight characters followed by a period and a three character extension. When naming your files, try to choose a memorable name that is easy to type. Choose filenames which make your documents distinctive and identifiable. WP will automatically put the appropriate three character extension on your filename to indicate this is a WP document.

If you have saved your document before, selecting File, Save or the Save button will save the revised document with the same name and path as that in the title bar and write over the original document. If you don't want to overwrite the original document, select File, Save As, then give the document a new name. This way you will have both the old and new versions of the document. This can be useful when you are not sure whether or not your revisions have improved the original document. When naming revisions, itís a good idea to keep the titles related (such as paraphrase.doc and paraphrase2.doc) so they are easy to locate.

Printing a Document

After creating, editing, and saving a document, you may want to print it. Select File, Print. You will see the Print dialog box with the current printer listed and other printing options. Make the appropriate selections and click Print or OK. If you click the Print icon on the Tool bar, the document will be printed to the default printer for the computer you are working at.

You may want to preview the document before you send it to the printer, especially if your printer is located in a remote location. Checking your document before you print may save you time and it will save paper, especially if you have to reprint an entire document because your header was incorrect. To check the location of your page numbers and header, for example, select File, Print Preview or click the Print Preview button on the Tool bar. You will see your document, including the headers and page numbers. After you have made sure that you do want to print the document without additional changes, select the File, Print or click the Print button from the Tool bar.

⚠ Always save your document before attempting to print it; if you do not, you may lose the document if something goes wrong in the print process.

Exiting WP

When you have finished editing one document and want either to open another document or to begin a new document, you should usually exit the current document. To do this, select File, Close. If the document has not been saved, you will see a WP dialog box asking if you want to save the document. If the document has been saved (the title bar gives the path and filename), the current document closes and you see an empty editing screen. You can now open another document or begin typing a new document.

If you open a new document without closing the current document, the new document window covers the old document window. When you close the second document, you will return to the first document.

When completely finished with a word processing session, you should exit WP and return to Win2000. After saving your work, select File, Exit, or click the Exit button on the right of the Title Bar. In the Computer Labs WP takes at least 30 seconds to complete writing information to your disk. You MUST wait until the light on the floppy drive comes on and goes off before removing your disk from the computer.

You now know how to load and exit WP, navigate in a document, insert and delete text, apply basic format changes to text, create a header, and save and print a document. In the next lesson you will learn about connecting to the Internet and using email.

Name _____

Section _____

1. If you're not certain that you want to open a particular file, how can you look at the file without actually opening it?

2. What is Typeover mode?

3. How do the Delete and Backspace keys differ in their actions in WP text?

4. In talking about filenames, what does an extension mean?

5. If you have just opened a document and you use the scroll bar to go to page 5 in that document, where will the cursor be positioned?

6. Give the steps for inserting a header on page 2 of your document.

7. How do you view a document before you print it?

8. List three ways of making a word bold.

9. How do you exit WP?

10. What is word wrap?

Lesson 3 — Connecting to the World

Computer networks today provide an amazing array of information and services. Some of these services, America Online for example, are operated by companies for profit just like other businesses. Many universities provide "free" access to educational and government networks as part of their research and teaching mission. In this brief introduction it is possible only to suggest the range of information and services available to you as a student at the university.

In this lesson you will learn about electronic mail, computerized library catalogs, and probably the most widely used computer information server in the world, the Internet and the World Wide Web (WWW).

To use the various services on the university computer network, you need an active account on the campus central computer system. Off campus you will need to access the university network by using a dial up or cable modem. For instructions about using the university's computer resources, go to http://www.d.umn.edu/itss/students/. Here you will learn how to set up your email account, change your password, use dial up networking, and find email addresses.

Using Email

Electronic mail allows you to send messages over the computer network to students, faculty, and staff on campus as well as to campuses across the United States and the world. You can send email to people in businesses and residences with Lotus Notes, Compuserve, America Online, Outlook, and similar programs if you know their electronic addresses.

To use electronic mail on campus, follow the instructions for using Mulberry, Outlook, Eudora, Netscape Mail, or IMP Webmil at http://www.d.umn.edu/itss/email/.

When you have opened the email program you want to use, fill in the address after the To. You need to know the person's email address, krisdon for example, for someone on campus. Just the personís name will not work. For people off campus, you also need to include the address of the computer the person has an account on. Usually the name and location are separated by an @ symbol: e.g., lrblake@aol sends email to Lucy Blake on America Online or drisdon@dialaccess.com sends email to Diana Risdon at her email address. To send a copy of the message automatically to another person, fill in the address on the cc: line. You can send a copy to yourself, for example, by typing your login on this line.

The Subject line will be displayed in the recipient's mail index; it has the obvious purpose of telling the receiver what your message is about. At this point type your message. When you have finished typing your message, check the spelling if your email program has a spell checker. When finished, mail the message.

Email Cautions

Email has become a very quick way to communicate with friends and associates. Several cautions need to be made about this convenient technology.

- Viruses are frequently transmitted through email attachments. Be very cautious about opening an email attachment from someone you donít know. The attachment may contain a virus that can damage not only your computer, but the computer network. All university computers run anti-virus software that can detect many of the email viruses. Anti-virus software is a good, although not infallible, protection for your computer system.

- Be careful about replying to and forwarding email. If you reply to a mailing list, your message will go to everyone on the mailing list, a result you may not have intended. Also be careful in forwarding email messages with attachments. One person received an email from a friend; she inadvertently forwarded the email to the entire company. Unfortunately, the email contained a virsus. The sender was immediately known in an unfavorable light.

- Use common sense in forwarding humor, graphics, and other information in email. Email is not private; because the university and corporations own their computer networks, they have the right and a legal responsibiility to monitor the networks. Be sensitive to the recepient's desire for privacy. Donít send chain letters, jokes, and other useless information to all your friends; this type of information clogs up the system and can irritate the recepients.

- Use the university email system for all university business, including communicating with your Composition instructor. With hundreds of students, your instructor does not have time to keep track of non-university email user names. University policy allows you to use the university email resources to communicate with non-university personnel; however, it is a good idea not to abuse this privilege by using the system in an excessive manner.

Library Catalog

Many libraries across the country now supply their catalogs on public computer networks, especially Internet. Most universities today provide access from on campus or over a modem to the local electronic catalog. In fact some libraries no longer maintain a physical card catalog at all. Many online library systems include electronic periodical indexes, reference sources, or even full-text periodicals, in addition to the catalog.

The Library Orientation session will show you how to use the university library catalog system.

Netscape

Netscape is a World Wide Web (WWW or W3) browser and viewer that allows you to access literally thousands of locations and millions of documents around the world. These documents may contain text, pictures, movies, and/or sound. You may not be able to view all of the pictures or play the sound because of limitations of a specific computer. Netscape attempts to minimize the detail that you need to know to navigate the Internet successfully by allowing you to make selections from menus by clicking on text, pictures, or icons. The program automatically reads the technical information, called the Universal Resource Locator (URL), associated with the information you request, makes the connection for you, and moves the text and pictures to your screen.

Netscape also takes you to some of the same places you can get to from other access points on the network. If you have a better way of getting where you need to go, you may use that after you have tried the pathways suggested here. To use Netscape select the Netscape icon, shown below.

Double clicking this icon automatically loads the UMD homepage. From this page you can go to many different information sources around the campus and the world. You will have to spend some time working with this system to see just how much is available through Netscape and the Internet. You may be able to collect information for your research projects here as well as explore the Information Superhighway.

Depending on how a particular screen is set, the UMD homepage (and many others) may not completely show in the window. To view suc-ceeding screens use the scroll bars to move down and up or left and right as needed, just as you do in any other Win2000 program. From the UMD homepage you can access network resources across campus and the world.

To use any of the items in a Netscape list, sim-ply click the line or icon when the cursor changes from an arrow to a hand. Once you have made a selection, you will see a series of messages at the bottom of the screen that tell you what is happening. Some of the locations may take up to several minutes to load because of traffic on the network or the presence of large graphics in the file. At times when many stu-dents are likely to be using Netscape, the sys-tem may be very slow.

The UMD homepage provides easy access to two important sources of research materials. First, the Library link connects you to the uni-versity Catalog and to the Electronic Resources, the indexes to thousands of reputable and even refereed printed serial and online publications. The second is the Search Internet, a link to UMD Search Engine Page, a list of about forty search engines for finding information on the WWW. It includes such useful choices as AltaVista, Lycos,

WebCrawler, Google, and Yahoo. These will con-
nect you to literally millions of documents from
around the world (some reliable, others idiosyn-
cratic or of dubious worth). The search engines
list results in different ways and may search different sets of files. The best one to use depends
on your specific topic and what kinds of documents you need. Many other services are available over the network. As with other complex
systems, it will take practice to use these
resources efficiently and effectively. Once you
have learned how to use them, they become a
powerful source of help and information for
research and writing.

As you work on your research project, become
familiar with the wealth of information available
to you by using the WWW, library catalogs, and
search engines.

Computing for College Writing

Lesson 4 — The Basics

When revising and editing your writing, you may be reluctant to make changes that are time consuming and boring when they force you to recopy or retype a revised version. With any good word processing program, you can accomplish many of these dreary tasks with a minimum of keystrokes. The highlight function is essential to this process, for it indicates a beginning and an end to a section of text. After highlighting a block of text, you can perform numerous functions on the text: move it, copy it, delete it, change capitalization, center it, make it flush right, spell check it, print it, save it on a disk, change its font, and, of course, boldface, italicize, or underline it.

Highlighting Text

To highlight text, position the cursor at the first character of the text to be selected, click and hold the left mouse button while dragging the mouse through the text you want marked, releasing the left mouse button when finished. Once you have highlighted the text, you are ready to give the computer additional instructions about what you want done by giving a second command. However, once text is highlighted, if you press the spacebar, the text will be deleted (this is when the undelete command of Edit, Undo is especially useful).

To select one word quickly with the mouse, position the mouse pointer on the word and click twice; for one sentence (or until the next period) in WordPerfect or a paragraph in Word, position the cursor anywhere in the sentence or paragraph and click three times; for an entire paragraph in WordPerfect, position the pointer anywhere in the paragraph and click four times. You may have to practice to get the right timing of the multiple clicks.

Cutting Text

An important editing function is the move function. You can move text by cutting it from its original location and pasting it in another location or by copying it and pasting in a different location. The only difference is that one actually moves the text, whereas the other copies a duplicate of the selected text in a different location. To move the highlighted text, select Edit, Cut, select the Cut button, or press Ctrl-x. The text disappears from the screen. Position the cursor at the location where you want to place the cut text, and then select Edit, Paste, select the Paste button, or press Ctrl-v. The text appears at the cursor location.

Copying Text

To copy text from one position to another in the same document, after highlighting the text select Edit, Copy, select the Copy button, or press Ctrl-c. The highlighted text remains on the screen, and Select remains in the Status Bar. Position the cursor where you want the text to be copied, and select Edit, Paste, select the Paste button, or press Ctrl-v. An exact copy of the highlighted text appears at the cursor position.

Another option is to copy selected text to
another file, either an existing file or a new one.
To copy to an existing file, first mark the passage to be copied and give the Copy command.
Then open the existing file and place Insertion
point (cursor) in the position where the marked
text is to be placed. Press the Paste button or
press Ctrl-v. To copy to a new file, begin by
marking the text to copy and giving the Copy
command. Then simply click the New Blank
Document icon on the Toolbar and press the
Paste button or press Ctrl-v. Donít forget to
Save your revised files before exiting from WP.

Deleting Text

To delete the highlighted text, press Delete or
Backspace. The marked text disappears. You
can also select Edit, Cut or press the Cut button
or press Ctrl-x.

If you highlight a block of text and press the
space bar, the highlighted text will be deleted.
You can recover it by selecting Edit, Undo. The
creators of WP had a specific function in mind
when the program was designed this way: quick
deletion of text. Unfortunately, most users are
surprised by the way this combination works.

Undo

If you decide that you did not want to delete the
text, immediately select Edit, Undo or press
Ctrl-z. WP remembers deletions you have made
by any method, highlight and delete, delete, or
backspace. If the deletion that appears highlighted on the screen is not the one you want,

select Edit, Undo again. Undo cancels the most recent change you made in your document. It will return deleted text to its original position. Just remember that if you gave WP a command that you did not want it to do, immediately select Edit, Undo or press Ctrl-z. An easy option

is to press the Undo button 🔄 on the Tool bar. If you decide that you do not want to undo, click

Redo 🔁 on the Tool bar to restore what you undid.

Changing Appearance of Text

In addition to changing the positioning of the actual text in your document, you can also use the highlight function to change the appearance of printed text. For example, after highlighting text, you can boldface, underline, italicize, or center it, as well as change it from lower to uppercase. You can also change its font (e.g., Times New Roman to Century Gothic), position (e.g., subscript or superscript characters), the style of the characters (e.g., shadow print, small caps, double underline, strikeout) or change the sizes of type.

Highlight the block of text you want to change with the mouse. When you have highlighted the text, select **B**, U, or *I* from the Tool bar, select Format, Font and make your selection in the Font dialog box, or press Ctrl-b, Ctrl-u, or Ctrl-i. The highlighted text will be boldfaced, under-lined, or italicized.

Using Flush Right

Another appearance feature that WP performs effortlessly is the Flush Right function. This function automatically aligns text so that any number of a series of lines will be flush to the right margin. For example, you might want your header to be in flush right format; it would look like the sample below:

James Dean Taylor, 007
COMP 1120, Sec. 106
Lesson Four

To position a line flush right, simply select the Right Justification (Align Right) button from the Tool bar. The cursor goes to the right margin; begin typing, and you will notice that the letters automatically jump to the left one character at a time. To end this function, select another justification button from the Tool bar.

Converting the case of characters can be especially useful if you have inadvertently turned the Caps Lock key on, if you need to capitalize key words in a title, or if you are revising headings within a text. After highlighting the string of words to be converted, press Edit, Convert Case (WordPerfect) or Format, Change Case (Word). Select the option you want.

You can also center a multi-line block. Like bold and underline, you have to highlight the text. Then select Center on the Tool bar.

Using Indent and Hanging Indent

Other appearance items you will want to use as you do your academic papers are the Indent and Hanging Indent functions of WP. When you are doing research papers, it may be necessary to quote blocks of text. The conventional practice for quoting a passage of five lines or more is to indent and single space the quotation. WP's Indent function takes care of this format problem while allowing your typing to word wrap. The Indent function moves each line of text of a paragraph an equal distance to the right from the left margin (known as Indent) or an equal distance in from both left and right margins (known as Double Indent). The Hanging Indent performs the same as an Indent, but it brings the first line back to the original left margin, usually used in bibliographic entries.

Indent, Double Indent, and Hanging Indent are all functions of Format, Paragraph. You may also find Format buttons on the Tool bar.

You now know the basics of manipulating text in your documents. In the next lesson you will learn more about handling online resources.

Lesson 5 — Handling Online Sources

Calling this chapter "Handling Online Sources" is a shorthand way of suggesting the many tasks, skills, and responsibilities that a researcher must command in bringing a project to a successful conclusion. The tasks range from the invention and discipline necessary to locate relevant, authoritative sources to the accurate recording of information essential to the purpose of the research project. The skills range from mastering printed and online indexes and bibliographies to the discovering of key terms and controlling of technology necessary for recording and producing texts for readers. The responsibilities range from the ensuring the honest and accurate treatment of evidence to a sustained effort to observe the ethics of persuasion and evaluation in an era characterized by manipulative communications media.

By now you should be familiar with the following principles for researchers:

- Be accurate
- Be complete in recording what you find
- Follow consistent procedures
- Keep track of your thinking as you work
- Be always skeptical and alert to the possibility of error, bias, or confusion
- Do your work once and do it right

Comparing Search Engines

Ann Raimes reports the president of the Association of College Research Libraries, William
Miller, as saying "Much of what purports to be
serious information [on the Web] is simply junk
— neither current, objective, nor trustworthy"
(KFW 73). Yet the Web search engines are
widely used, and we cannot justly reject or
quarrel with them without firsthand knowledge
of using them and their functions.

For a quick but revealing exposure to the first
four sites on Raimes' list (65-66), the lab exercise uses one of the key phrases in the sample
research paper "A New Way to Look at Y2K":
Time Bomb 2000. The aims of the comparison
are simple, yet they should prove to be revealing. An obvious aim is to become familiar
enough with Web search engines to use them
confidently even if with some justified suspi-
cions. Secondly, your confidence can grow only
when you have had enough experience to know
which sites are most likely to contain the kinds
of information you seek. A few minutes spent
with a site proves very revealing (as long as you
can apply some predictable criteria). A third
aim, therefore, is to suggest a few simple criteria that promise some rough measures of the
sites' effectiveness and reliability.

What this lesson will do is to give you some
experience in bringing together laboratory train-
ing and practice with the practical job of finding
and evaluating source materials relevant to the
research project that you propose to develop in
your composition course. In the process of

doing so we intend to reinforce your under-standing of the kinds of resources available to you, including some of their strengths and weaknesses.

We propose using these criteria for predicting a site's effeceiveness and reliability:

- Ease of accessing the Web site in a few sim-ple steps. For example, can you move easily from Netscape to the Web search engine?

- Speed of accessing the search results. With a watch you can easily time the seconds or minutes that pass to access a search engine. The results might be interesting, but they may also reveal little about the performance of a particular Web site or search engine.

- Ease of use. Is the opening screen (or home page) of the Web site easy to interpret, and are its instructions clear? Or must you sort through irrelevant information and adver-tisements for products and services to find what you seek?

Additional criteria for predicting a site's effec-tiveness and reliability:

- The number of "hits" using a given keyword, phrase, or sets of terms. You will probably be surprised at some of the numbers this exercise produces, but counts alone may be all but irrelevant. For example, one search for information on the graphic artist M. C. Escher produced about 2,000 "hits." The trouble was that most of them were advertisements for products using some of Escher's designs: T-shirts, coffee mugs, playing cards, postcards, note pads, inexpensive reproductions, calendars, and the like.

- Exactness of match to the designated keyword or phrase. Does the search engine restrict the matches just to the terms you specify in their same order? The words in the phrase "time bomb 2000" can easily be used in at least six different ways consistent with the grammar of the English language (to say nothing of all possible permutations). This criterion usually provides helpful results.

- Quality of the information identified. This criterion is the all important one, which we shall address when considering Internet resources most likely to be productive.

Full-Text Articles and Documents

The most authoritative sources available online are generally those available in full-text formats. These are typically the products of scholarly and professional organizations of almost all fields and disciplines, such fields as those of the Association of Computing Machinery, the National Academy of Sciences, Project Muse (arts, humanities, law, history, and some sciences), ABI Inform (business), LEXIS-NEXIS (law), and JSTOR (selected titles in ethnic studies, history, literature, law and politics), SIAM (mathematics), Ideal Academic Press (science and technology), and Chadwyck-Healy Literary

Databases (British and American literary texts). Additional databases provide full-text articles from Encyclopedia Britannica and selected newspapers as well as studies in music, microbiology, physics, computing and telecommunications.

Just as all online resources are not created equal, neither are the resources available in full-text databases. A professional bibliographer would distinguish at least three classes of full-text sources in order of descending authority:

- verbatim image of the source text

- edited and paginated source text

- edited source text

Verbatim Image of the Source Text

These texts reproduce a virtual graphic image of the original source text. This means that ideally they reproduce every feature of each original page, including page numbers and any headers, footers, graphics, tables, footnotes, variations in fonts, and even typographical errors as published in the source text. When displayed and printed using such programs as Adobe Acrobat, the pages cannot often be readily distinguished from the product of a photocopier. They often lack even the URL usually printed on the top right hand comer of pages printed while using other Internet sources.

Their authority derives from their being graphic images of the original text, which means that nobody has an opportunity to tinker with the source text in any way. Readers know exactly what the original looked like, as much as an electronic device can reproduce a printed page. Hence you know on exactly what page the author makes a claim or analyzes a piece of evidence. If an essay begins with an epigram, you know from its position and format just what its purpose is. Because such texts are so close to the original, researchers can provide complete information demanded by style manuals, such as the MLA or Chicago. But they must also be scrupulous in documenting their access to them, lest readers be misled about the authority of the source.

The only disadvantages of using such sources, when they are available, are probably economic. To use them researchers may have to download and install Adobe Acrobat or a similar program. University students, faculty, and staff may have access to Acrobat, but some of the services assess a connection fee for each use. Because graphic images are usually slower to process online than verbal ones, online costs can be significant, especially if a researcher must pay long-distance telephone costs while using a slow modem. Reference librarians recommend the low-quality text option while downloading the image to Acrobat to save time and money. The low-quality texts are fully readable, but the characters and graphic details in them are somewhat fuzzy. They look like fuzzy ink jet output when placed along side the product of a good Postscript printer.

Edited and Paginated Source Text

Sources in this category typically derive from printed sources, so they can partially satisfy the bibliographer's demand that citations describe some tangible object. Their formats, however, look like a product derived from using a scanner and a good Optical Character Recognition program (OCR) to convert graphic images to individual characters. Page design, the choice of fonts, the labeling of blocks of discourse, distinctions between body text and notes, the treatment of tables and illustrations all depend upon the performance of the scanner and the skills of the editor responsible for preparing the text for the Web pages. Anyone who has used an OCR knows that even the best of them can produce garbled texts, and that illustrations and tables may be lost.

A good editor can produce a verbal text very close to the original, but it cannot claim to substitute for it. Usually the services presenting these texts provide notes to inform readers about any necessary changes or omissions. The best of them indicate the date or dates on which the text was entered or edited, and editors may be identified by name. A reader, however, has no way of knowing how close to the original the text may be.

Sources in this category leave the researcher even less informed about the original text than the previous one. Basic bibliographical information is always provided, but the citation may indicate only the starting page number and the number of pages in the original. They provide, therefore, no means to indicate the page on which a particular piece of information or argument occurs.

Because network programs and connections may be set up differently, as well as printers connected to the networks, the number of pages printed from these full-text sources can provide no clue to original pagination. If the original text has section or paragraph numbers, these may be used to make references more precise; this practice is more common in the sciences than in the humanities and the arts. Some instructors require their students to count and number the paragraphs in unpaginated texts. This enables researchers to narrow the references to sources. Unless those numbering paragraphs agree upon conventions for handling the block indentation of long quotations and other special formats, no two people are likely to count paragraphs in a long essay exactly the same way. Nevertheless, this is a practice we encourage when citing texts that lack page numbers.

Establishing the Reliability of Sources

This lesson emphasizes criteria and procedures that are applicable to questions of the authorship and authority, the accuracy and verifiability, and the currency of source materials available on the Internet. Because libraries everywhere depend increasingly upon electronic resources, their patrons must become ever more conscious of both the benefits and shortcomings of their intangible resources.

In conducting searches for information and selecting source materials, give preference to the works listed in indexes and bibliographies produced by professional and scholarly organizations that work in the field of your research topic. Most of the publications identified in the master lists of serial bibliographies require peer reviews, and final approval of articles for publication usually requires the consent of an editorial board. Many Web sites, alas, deserve William Miller's characterization of them.

Authority and the Author's Affiliations

In beginning your research you probably have few clues to answer the question of exactly who even a known author is. You cannot expect to know much about an author until you have studied closely what the author has written. But you have at your fingertips the resources you need to answer this revealing question: What has the author accomplished, participated in, or completed that signals credibility, prestige, or professional recognition? A closely related question is this one: What are the author's affiliations? These questions are relevant to your needs because you care less who the author is than what the author has done.

Finding out about an Author

An illustration of the process of learning something about an unfamiliar author will show what you, too, can do. Recent teaching of late Renaissance masques aroused curiosity about recent studies of the genre.

- Conduct a search: Through SearchBank we reached Infotrac and entered the keyword "masque." One of the dozen entries called up by this search was this one:

  Johnson, Nora. "Body and Spirit, Stage and Sexuality in The Tempest." ELH 64 (1997): 683-701.

- Print a full-text copy of the article (available through SearchBank) and read it.

- Examine the article for evidence of its substance and its author's abilities and stature. It is an unpaginated full-text copy of a substantial article, well-documented, in a prestigious publication from a noted center of literary and historical studies, The Johns Hopkins University. ELH (the acronym and now the title of what was English Literary History). The journal began publication in about 1933. The author proves to be widely read and to know current scholarship, criticism, and theory relevant to the subject. She teaches at Swarthmore College, a prestigious liberal arts college in Pennsylvania.

- Use the Arts & Humanities Citation Index - accessible through Web of Science - to see how her work has been received. The index cites no references to her work but it lists four of her publications since 1996. They all appear in sound, refereed journals: Shakespeare Quarterly, Shakespeare Studies, ELH, and Theatre Journal. She appears to be a young teacher-scholar who is making an excellent start in her career.

- Confirm inferences about her performance: Check authors indexes of the World Shakespeare Bibliography and the MLA Intemational Bibliography.

Both internal evidence and public records suggest that Nora Johnson is establishing herself as a reputable writer in Renaissance studies. The citation indexes provide a quick way to gain an overview of a scholar's or scientist's performance.

Accuracy and Verifiability

- Check to see if a source includes a bibliography, a list of references, works cited, or suggestions for further reading. The inclusion of such lists usually indicates that a writer is familiar with relevant scholarship and the development of studies in the subject. Their content may show the author's particular focus. Remember that such lists and references in the body text may also provide leads to other helpful works.

- Note the ways in which the author cites, analyzes, and documents evidence relevant to the controlling argument and the claims. Note especially the care taken in providing warrants to link evidence to the position being developed.

Currency

- When researching scholarly, scientific, and technical subjects, make sure that the dates of your sources reflect up-to-date knowledge, principles, and procedures. You can often identify works considered central to the study of a subject by starting with recent studies and noting the references that recur in notes and lists of references or works cited. Be skeptical about studies that fail to take into account recent work.

- When examining online resources, note if they include two dates: 1) the date on which a particular record was posted in the database, and 2) the date on which you accessed the record and took notes on it, copied it, or printed it. If the record has been revised, note also the date of the revision (and the name of the responsible party if this information is given).

You should now have a better understanding of how to handle research sources for your research project. The next lesson will feature several very powerful word processing tools.

Lesson 6 — Tools

You now know how to manipulate text using functions in WP essential for revising and editing your writing. You can insert text, delete text, or move or copy text from one place to another. WP has several methods for deleting text which are quicker than Backspace or Del which remove only one character at a time. We will also look at several WP tools that can help you improve the quality of your writing.

Deleting Text

You have already seen that you can delete a block of text by highlighting the text and pressing Delete or Backspace to delete the block. This method of deleting, however, does not allow you to use the Paste function to recover the deletion in another location. You can, however, use the Undo function if you have just deleted the text. Other methods of deleting text exist that you may prefer to use. Another method of deleting a block is to highlight the text and then select Edit, Cut or the Cut button, or press Ctrl-x. Each of these methods allows you to paste the deleted information in the same or in a different location if you decide you did not want to delete it. Just select the Paste button on the Tool bar or press Ctrl-v.

If you want to delete one word, you can use the Ctrl-Backspace combination. This two key combination deletes the word at the cursor whether the cursor is at the beginning, middle, or end of the word. The entire word will be deleted.

Although you cannot paste the word deleted by this method, you can use Undo to restore the text if used soon after the deletion.

Using Spell Checkers

Not only is WP powerful for manipulating text; it also is a time saver in proofreading for spelling errors. With Spell Check, you can check the spelling of your document against WP's dictionary. Spell Check mainly checks for spelling, double occurrence of words, words with mixed upper- and lowercase letters, and words with numbers. Since the Spell Check dictionary contains only 100,000+ words (a good desk dictionary may contain 250,000 words), it will not contain all possible words in a document nor will it identify correctly spelled words used incorrectly, for example, *threw* used instead of *through*, *its* for *it's*, or *form* for *from*.

⚠ Before using Spell Check, always SAVE THE DOCUMENT you want to spell check. Follow the same principle before printing a file, changing floppy disks, or running a grammar checker.

To check the spelling in your document, open the document you want to check. Select Spell

Checker 📖 or Spelling and Grammar ✔ on the Tool bar. The Spell Check dialog box appears toward the bottom of your screen over your document text screen.

Spell Check looks at each word in your document; when it finds a word its dictionary does not recognize, it highlights the word in the text, places the word not found in the dialog box, and gives suggested replacements. If the suggested word is correct, select the Change or Replace button. If the word is not in the WP dictionary or the misspelling is unusual, no replacement choices will appear to choose from. If you know that the word is spelled correctly (a proper name for example) you can select ignore to tell the program to skip this occurrence and high-light the next, or tell the program to skip all occurrences of this word in the entire document.

If no choices appear for the word, but you know that it is misspelled, click the word in the docu-ment editing screen. You will be able to edit the word directly in the document.

After you have checked all the words Spell Check asks you if you want to close Spell Check. If you select Yes or OK, the dialog box disap-pears and the full editing screen reappears. Then be sure to SAVE THE SPELL CHECKED DOCUMENT. Otherwise all the changes you have made with the Spell Checker will be lost.

Using Style Checkers

To this point, you have mastered some of the powerful tools available to you in WP. You can enter, manipulate, and store information, and use Spell Check. However, you may have found that WP has not actually improved your writing. To analyze your writing style and aid you in improving your writing, you need to use a dif-ferent software program, a style checker.

Although with WP you may produce adequately spelled, correctly formatted essays, you may need to look at the stylistic and rhetorical choices you made in your writing to improve the quality of your written communication. For example, WP would not prevent you from writing the following sentence: "Style checkers will only read the original file and show you the potential problems it find, but won't make any changes or create any marked or corrected copy." Specifically designed to aid you in improving your style, style checkers can be valuable tools in proofreading, editing, and revising your writing.

Style checkers function as a proofreader and as a grammar and usage checker.

- As a proofreader, style checkers check spelling, punctuation, and capitalization. It will note doubled words or punctuation marks and omitted punctuation marks, particularly in paired marks such as " ", [ ], and ( ).

- As a grammar checker, it checks for subject-verb agreement, pronoun agreement, fragments, possessives, articles, homonyms, vague adverbs and adjectives, split infinitives, one-sentence paragraphs, passive voice constructions, etc. It can provide additional information if you need help in making a correct choice.

- As a usage checker, style checkers look for clumsy, trite, misused, pretentious, wordy, or redundant word choices and give alternatives.

Some style checkers (e.g., WordPerfect's Grammatik) provide a readability index and a statistical analysis of the number of paragraphs, average paragraph length, number of sentences, average length of sentences, number of passives, long and short sentences, total word count, and the number of prepositions. The readability formula provides you some sense of the difficulty of the text. Using the average length of your sentences, the percentage of long words, and the number of syllables per word, Grammatik figures the Flesch-Kincaid Grade Level that gives a readability score roughly indicating the average number of school years a reader needs to understand your document. To run Grammatik, click Spell Checker on the Tool bar, and select the Grammatik tab. Follow the instructions in the dialog box.

Word is usually set to automatically check spelling and grammar as you type your papers. It allows you to change the writing style against which you want to check your writing. Word highlights potential misspelled words with a **red** wavy line, potential grammatical mistakes with a **green** wavy line. Click the highlighted word to see the potential suggestions. To accept the suggestion, click the suggestion and it will replace the highlighted word.

You can customize most style checkers to have them not check for certain grammatical mistakes or to automatically correct mistakes.

Cautions about Style Checkers

Style checkers can be helpful in identifying some of the potential rhetorical problems in our writing. They are, however, not always accurate. For example, occasionally Grammatik will incorrectly identify the subject of a clause and ask for a verb to agree in number with this subject. If you were to accept the style checkerís comment, you would actually insert a mistake in an already correct clause. Consider these sentences from a draft of the *College Writing* textbook.

> We think that government, like every other contrivance of human wisdom, from the highest to the lowest, is likely to answer its main end best when it is constructed with a single view to that end.

In this sentence, Grammatik comments, "If We is the subject of the verb is, try making them agree in number." Of course, government functions as the subject of is, not We. To make a change would be a mistake. Similar to this is the following sentence:

> Restate the main point of a passage in your own words.

About this sentence, Grammatik comments, "If main is the subject of the verb point, try making them agree in number." Here, again, main is an adjective to the noun point. Grammatik does not recognize the imperative verb Restate, for it later states, "This may not be a complete sentence."

Computing for College Writing

Grammatik also incorrectly points out the following sentence as a potential problem.

Look for a statement in the passage that sums up its author' s main point.

Grammatik comments, "An article or other modifier usually precedes the word point. Check also for errors in hyphenation, possessive form, capitalization, and modifier." In this case, author's is the determiner of the noun phrase and main is a modifier of the head noun point. Grammatik, however, does not recognize that the problem derives from the extra space after the apostrophe.

Style checkers can be customized to suit your individual needs; for example, you can disable the speller, particularly if you have already used WP's Spell Check; or you can insert individual phrases you tend to overuse into the phrase dictionary. You can set the preferences to compare your document to various writing styles, such as report or advertising style. As you become a better writer, you will be able to discontinue using some style checker features.

Managing Files

As you begin to write more frequently with the computer, you need to know how to manage your files. Since you will probably be keeping all your work on a floppy disk, you want to know how to make backup copies of your important files. Making backup copies means copying information from one place to another so that you have a duplicate of your files in case something happens to your floppy disk. Although you can use several different methods of managing your files, we will review features of Windows Explorer that serve this purpose.

To use the Windows Explorer, click Start, select Programs, Accessories, Windows Explorer. You will see the Explorer window.

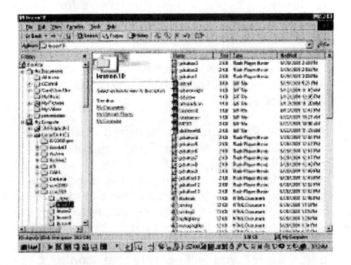

Explorer Tool Bar

The Explorer Tool Bar allows you to navigate, search, copy, move, and delete files and folders, undo, and change the display of the Explorer Window. Note that clicking the Folders button or clicking the X to the right of Folders in the left column eliminates the left column of the screen.

Current Folder

The folder displayed in the right column is indicated in the Address box, as well as highlighted
in the Folders section of the screen. If you have
clicked the Folders button on the Tool bar and
do not see the left column, click Folders again to
restore the left column. Clicking the down arrow
in the Address box shows you the drive and
directory structure.

Folders

The left column represents the file structure of
the selected drive and the other drives on the
computer. A + in front of a drive or folder
(directory) indicates that more levels of folders
(directories and subdirectories) exist on that
drive. At the top of the tree you will usually see
Desktop and My Computer, followed by a list of
all the other drives and folders where you can
store your files. The + indicates that more levels
exist in hierarchy of drives and folders on the
disk.

Folders in the Current Directory

The right column represents the file structure of
the selected drive or directory. Folders that may
contain additional folders and files are listed
first. Double clicking the folder will display its
contents.

Files in the Current Directory

The right column shows all the files in the currently selected folder (the one highlighted in the

left column and indicated in the Address box). If
you have Details turned on in Views, you can
see the file name, file size, type of file, and date
last modified. You can change the view to a list,
thumbnails, or icons. Single clicking a file displays details about the file and a thumbnail
graphic of the file in the middle of the Explorer
screen, if available. Double clicking the file will
launch the program the file is associated with,
e.g., a Word document will launch Word and a
gif graphic will launch Photoshop.

Changing Drives and Folders

When you want to change the current drive,
select (click once) the new drive from the list
displayed in the tree in the left column. Now the
right column displays the information for the
new drive.

When you want to change folders (directories or
subdirectories), click once on the folder you
want to see. The item you selected is displayed
in the columns.

Create a New Folder

You may want to store all your files for your
composition class in a folder called COMP and all
your files for philosophy in a folder called
PHILO. To create these folders (directories) on
your floppy disk or on a hard disk while in
Explorer, highlight the drive you want the folder
in, select File, New, Folder. Type in the name of
the folder, comp for example, in the highlighted
box automatically created in the file list. You will
now have a root directory (A:\ or C:\) with one

folder, comp. Now you can save all your composition papers on your floppy disk, but you will have to remember to tell the computer to save the file to A:\comp\filename. If you donít put the folder name in the path, your file will probably be saved in some directory you do not expect, not your comp directory.

Each program in Win2000 may be set to save files in a different default folder, even if you opened the file from your floppy disk. Be sure to note the path for these default folders.

Folder and File Names

Win2000 allows a wide range of possibilities for folder and file names, but you need to use some common sense and caution with long names. If you attempt to use files or disks with long names or names with spaces in them on a computer running Windows 3.1, all of the long names will be shortened to fit the naming conventions of Windows 3.1 which does not allow long names. You may discover that you can no longer tell which file is which. Also if you have to run Scandisk because Win2000 failed, you will discover that all the long names have been arbitrarily shortened. We suggest that you follow the Windows 3.1 rules as filenames: the name can be up to eight characters and the extension can be up to three characters. Generally the name should start either with a number or letter and should not contain punctuation marks (except the . between the name and the extension).

Remember, if you should need help retrieving a file, you will be asked the fileís name. Donít name your file anything you might later be embarrassed to tell your instructor or a lab consultant.

Backup Folders and Files

Familiarizing yourself with the backup processes and using them often will help ensure your work is safe and accessible. Unfortunately students often forget to do these simple procedures and lose data as a result. Despite precautions we all may take, disks do get ruined.

One simple way to backup your entire disk is simply to copy it in its entirety to another disk. With one click, select the appropriate drive for your disk (generally A:). Right click the drive, and then chose Copy Disk. You will get a dialog box with the available drives to which to copy your drive, usually A: and a Zip drive. The computer will read all the information on your source disk and will prompt you to enter your destination disk. Simply eject the original source disk and replace it with the destination disk.

Remember, though, that any data existing on your destination disk prior to copying will be erased.

If your prefer to backup selected files from your disk, rather than the entire disk, youíll want to use Explorer. This is a two step procedure wherein you copy your files from the floppy to the hard drive, and then from the hard drive to your backup floppy. To begin, place your floppy disk to copy in the drive, and in Explorer select the appropriate drive as the current drive. You will now see the list of the files on the floppy in the right column of Explorer. Select the files you want to copy by highlighting them.

- To select multiple **contiguous** files (files all in a row), select the first file, hold down the Shift key, and select the last file, then release. All files between the first and the last selected are highlighted.

- To select multiple, **non-contiguous** files (those not next to each other), select the first file, hold down the Ctrl key, and select the remaining files, then release. All selected files will be highlighted.

Once you have selected the files, position your mouse in the highlighted portion of the right column. Hold the left mouse button down and drag the file icon(s) to an appropriate folder on the C: drive, then release (a temp folder generally works well if it is sufficiently empty). Your files will be copied. You can also select the files, then click Copy To on the Tool Bar, and select the appropriate folder on the C: drive.

⚠ If you forget to copy your files from the C: drive in public computer labs, other students will be able to access them.

Now that your files are on C:, it's time to place them on your backup disk. Eject your original disk and insert your destination disk. Click on the appropriate folder in C: (the place youíve just put your files) and all the files in this folder will appear in the right hand column. Highlight your files in the same manner you just did, then click Move To on the Tool Bar. Select the floppy drive in My Computer and click OK. After the files are copied, click on the destination diskís icon in the left column to ensure the files really are there.

⚠ If you use Copy To, be sure to go to the C: drive and delete your files.

Moving Files

Win2000 makes a distinction between moving and copying. Copying means just that; make a copy in another location. Move means to make a copy in another location and then delete the files in the original location. You can do either of these function by dragging files with the mouse. Also, Win2000 functions differently when you drag a folder or file to a different drive than when you drag it to another folder on the same drive. If you drag files from one drive to another, Explorer will make a copy of the file. If you drag files from one folder to another on the same drive, Explorer will move (not copy) the file.

To move files from C:\comp to C:\critical analysis, for instance, simply select (left click) the files and drag them to C:\critical analysis.

Explorer will automatically remove the files from
C:\comp. To move files from drive C: to drive A:
you will need to hold down either the Shift
(Move) or Ctrl (Copy) key as you drag them or
Win2000 will simply make a copy of them. If
you drag files with the right mouse button,
Explorer displays a menu of options, Move Here,
Copy Here, Create Shortcut(s) Here, and Can-
cel. Using this makes clear exactly what you are
about to do. Before you perform any of these
options, you must change to the other mouse
button, so you have time to reconsider the
choice you have made.

Cautions about File Management

Two warnings are especially relevant at this
point. First, it is never a good idea to leave your
documents on a public lab computer. Second,
copying files is always safer than moving them.
If a computer malfunctions during the copy procedure, a copy of the document remains in one
of the locations, usually the original one. If a
malfunction occurs during a move procedure,
you might be left with a good copy in neither.
Just remember to go back and delete a file from
its original location after copying a file from a
public lab computer.

If Explorer finds a file by the same name as
a file you are copying or moving, it will ask you
if you want to replace the file. The file data, filename, bytes, and date created are displayed for
both files. This helps prevent accidentally writing over a newer file.

Delete Files

If you want to clean up your disk and delete
unused or unneeded files, you can easily delete
them with Explorer. Select the drive where the
files are located to display the file listing. Select
the files you want to delete. Press the Del key.
Win2000 will not ask you if you want to delete
the files. You will see a graphic of file folders
going into the Recycle Bin.

Now you should be able to use some of the powerful tools of WP and Win2000, tools that can
help you improve your spelling and style. In
addition being able to use Windows, using
Explorer properly and backing up your work frequently should prevent you from losing any
important information because you didnít make
a backup copy of your disk.

Lesson 7 — Advanced Format

You can now use WP to produce standard documents. However, you will likely have occasion to change the preset (default) settings in WP. You may be word processing a letter of application for a job, for example, and you want the letter centered top to bottom with larger margins than the preset 1" from the left and right edges of the page. The ability to change these options gives you the flexibility not only to manipulate the text within the document but also to change the appearance of the printed page. Many of these changes are simple to make using the Ruler, Format menu options, or the Tool bar.

Margins

When you are making changes to the default settings of margins or tabs, you will want to have the Ruler turned on. Select View, Ruler. You will see a ruler with the margin settings, inch markings for your paper size, and tab setting.

When you are finished, simply select View, Ruler again to turn it off.

WP provides multiple ways to change marginsó from the Menu Bar, with the function keys, or by simply dragging lines around on the screen. Very precise settings are most easily done in the dialog boxes. The WP default margins for a standard 8 1/2" by 11" sheet of paper are 1î from all sides (Word has a 1.25" right and left margin as the default). To change these default margin settings, position the cursor where you want the change to begin, and select File, Page Setup.

You will see the Page Setup dialog box. Type in the new margins, select Apply to: This point forward in Word, and select OK. The margins will be changed at the cursor position for the rest of the document. Thus, if you want several different margins in your document, set the initial margins at the beginning of the document (or use the preset left and right margins). When you want to change margins, position the cursor where the change should begin, and change the margins. When finished with this new margin setting, change it again to the original (or another) setting.

A quick way to change the margins is to turn the Ruler on, select the right, left, top, or bottom margin and drag it to the new margin location.

Reducing the top margin in WordPerfect improves the appearance of the printed page when using headers (it will also save paper). From the Page Setup dialog box, first reduce the top margin to 0.41î. Then select Insert, Header/ Footer, Header A, Create. Enter the full header on the first page of your text then close the header. Move the cursor a few lines into the second page of your text. Select Insert, Header/ Footer, Header A, Discontinue. Return to page two of your document. Select Format, Header, Header B, Create, and type in a new header with just your name and the page number flush right (for example, Risdonovich - 2). This modified header will now appear on pages two and following until your document ends or you discontinue it.

Tabs

Occasionally you may desire to change the default tab settings of every ¾" across the line. To change the tab settings, position the cursor in the text where you want the tab settings changed, select Format, Line, Tab Set (or Format, Tabs in Word). You will see the Tab Set dialog box with the current tab settings listed and outlining the choices you can make.

Notice that in WordPerfect the preset tabs can be described in two ways: as relative to the left margin or absolute to the left edge of the paper. This means that with a 1" margin, the relative tabs will have the tab at the 1" left margin called 0", whereas the absolute tabs will have it called 1". WordPerfect's ruler is an absolute ruler; Word, on the other hand, uses a relative ruler, meaning that the inches marked on the ruler are always in reference to the left margin.

You can choose several different types of tabs.

- Left tabs are normal tabs that reposition the cursor at the tab position; anything you type moves to the right.

- Center tabs reposition the cursor at the tab position and center anything you type.

- Right tabs reposition the cursor at the tab position; anything you type moves to the left (similar to Flush Right).

- Dot Left, Center, and Right tabs produce a line of ..... (dot leaders) to the tab position.

- Dot Decimal tabs align tabs at the decimal, most often used in columns of numbers.

If you want to use dot leaders in a Table of Contents, for example, position a Dot Right tab at the position on the right margin where you want the page numbers. After you press the dot right tab, the leaders appear and everything you type will be right aligned, thus keeping your numbers even on the right margin.

A quick way to delete tabs is to select the tab you want to delete on the Ruler, and drag it off the Ruler. You can also move the tabs on the Ruler by selecting them and dragging them left or right to the position you want.

Hyphenation

An important feature that changes the appearance of the printed document is hyphenation. WP's default settings have hyphenation turned off. However, to even up the right margins, you can have WP hyphenate your text. This feature is a Tools, Language, Hyphenation feature. You can manually hyphenate a document after you have finished editing it, or you can have WP automatically hyphenate while you are creating the document.

WP gives its best guess at the correct hyphenation by using a set of rules to place the
hyphens in the words. If it cannot hyphenate
according to its rules, it places you in a dialog
box and asks you where to put the hyphen. If,
however, you do not want to hyphenate the
word, select Ignore Word or No, and the entire
word wraps to the next line.

Justification

Another way to control the look of the margins
is justification, meaning all lines are even on the
right, on the left, or on both sides of the page.
To enable right justification, position the cursor
where you want the justification to begin, click
the Justification button on the Tool bar. If you
select Full justification, everything from this
point on will be right-margin and left-margin
justified. Left justification aligns text to the left
margin, leaving a ragged right, while right justification aligns text to the right, leaving a ragged
left.

Page Break

WP is preset to insert a soft page break automatically when you have typed in enough text
to fill a page. However, you may wish to start a
separate section of your essay (Works Cited, for
example), on a new page. To do this, insert a
hard page break to force the printer to start
printing on a new page (don't just hit enter until
you get to a new page). Position the cursor at
the place where you want a new page to begin.
Press Ctrl-Enter or select Insert, Break, Page
break (or Insert, New Page in WordPerfect). A

new page appears. To delete a hard page break, position the cursor immediately before or after the page break line, and press Del or Back-space.

Fonts

After mastering the preceding changes in for-mat, you should be able to produce various doc-uments with different margins and tabs. Depending upon the printer you are using, you can also change the size and appearance of the type used in printing your documents. Available foreign alphabets include Cyrillic (Russian), Ara-bic, Hebrew, Japanese, and Greek. Other sets provide the diacritical marks of various alpha-bets, as well as the International Phonetic Alphabet. Here are some different fonts:

Wingding characters look like this:. ♋ ♌ ♍ ♎ ♏ ♐

Bookman Old Style is a comparatively wide font with serifs.

News Gothic is a narrow sans serif font.

Comic Sans MS mixes alignment on the world.

Brush Script isn't very readable. Is Palace better?

Garamond would make a good font for a greeting card.

Jokerman attempts to be funny.

To see if your printer supports changes in font size or appearance, move the cursor to where you want to change the font, select Format,

Font, to see the list of fonts available for your printer. In the Font dialog box, select the desired font, point size (the higher the number, the larger the font), appearance, and color, and select OK. Everything from this point forward will be in the new font. To return to the original font (or another one), position the cursor where the change should begin, select Format, Font, and make the appropriate changes.

You can also select the font and point size from the Tool bar.

Printers

If your current printer does not support the font changes you want but you have access to one that does, you will have to select a different printer in WP to be able to print these different fonts. To select a different printer, select File, Print. The down arrow for the Current Printer shows the available printers. Select the printer you want, then click the Print button. The document will now be printable on the new printer.

By the time you have studied this lesson and completed the exercises, you will be able to produce professional-quality printed documents. Remember that the menus and Help screens can lead you to most of the information contained in this lesson, so you need not memorize long lists of commands and procedures. Just remain alert to the information always before you on the screen.

Lesson 7 - Advanced Format

You now should have a fairly good command of WP; you can use both the basic and advanced formatting functions of your word processing program. In the next lesson you will learn how to incorporate graphics, tables, and columns into your documents.

Lesson 8 — Beyond Plain Text

WP has several advanced features that can help you communicate complex information more effectively than with words alone. These featuresó graphics, tables, and columnsórequire some patience in learning how to use them. Once you have used them, you will find that they can increase the range of tools you as a writer have at your disposal.

Graphics

WP provides a range of graphics capabilities that can be used to enhance documents. The graphics features of WP allow you to create Text Boxes into which you put text and then manipulate the box and text; to import graphics and digital photographs from other programs such as paint and clip art packages and the WWW; to draw lines; and to create equations. In this brief introduction to graphics we can only suggest the range of possibilities. Combined with other graphics programs, WP enables you to produce a wide variety of complex images and page designs.

Text Boxes

Text Boxes can be shaded, rotated, and surrounded by different types of lines (or no lines at all). Below is a text box with a graphic image and text. This text box has neither shading or a lines around it. Surrounding text is interrupted by the text box; you can have your text wrap around the text box.

You can delete a tab by dragging it off the ruler.

To create a Text box, select Text Box from the Tool bar. You can enter text, set text attributes, add lines, shading, and fill, and rotate the box and text. WP provides automatic numbering and caption options for a text box. To edit the properties of your text box, right click the box and select the options from the pop up menu.

Image Box

In addition to using text boxes, you may find that the Image box is the most flexible. Here you retrieve preexisting graphics, capture computer screens, or scan images into an Image box. After you have retrieved the image you want, you can modify its size, shape, and position in your text. Below is a graphic from a digital camera, a Word clipart photo, and a WordPerfect clipart graphic.

To retrieve an image, select Insert, Picture (Graphics in WordPerfect), or select Insert Clipart or Picture from the Tool bar. Choose a file from the WP list of graphics files or select another image from a clipart package, for example. The image appears on the screen in your document. You can now move the graphic by clicking on it; when you see the four-pointed arrow you can drag the whole figure around the screen to the location where you want the graphic. You can resize the graphic by selecting it and pointing the mouse at one of the corners of the graphic until you get a two-pointed arrow; hold the mouse button down while you shrink or stretch the box.

Lines

Occasionally you will want to position a horizontal or vertical line in your document (a resume, for example) in which you want a horizontal line separating your name from the rest of the resume. Vertical lines are often used to separate columns in multiple column newsletters.

To create a line, select Line from the Graphics or Draw Tool Bar. You can change the length, thickness, shading, color, and position of the line by selecting the line, clicking the right mouse button, and selecting Edit Line or Format AutoShape.

Tables

You may have occasion to use a table in your papers. For example, you have found interesting data relating to your research topic that would be clearer to your intended audience if it were presented in a table. Other times, to get rows of information aligned you may find a table without lines around it may help you to improve the appearance of your paper. Either way, tables can be a handy method to organize information.

If you are going to include a table in your document, you may want to open Tables Tool Bar. Simply point the mouse at the current Tool bar, press the right mouse button. Select Tables.

Word's Tables and Boarders Tool Bar

WordPerfect's Tables Tool Bar

To create a Table at the point you want to insert a table, select Table, Insert or Insert, Table. In the dialog box, define the number of columns (vertical) and the number of rows (horizontal) you want in your table. You will see a blank table at the cursor position with the number of columns and rows you selected, such as the one on the next page with three columns and four rows.

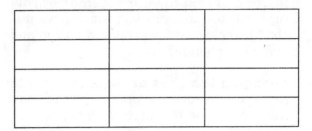

With the cursor in any of the cells, type the information you want in your table. To move to the next cell, press Tab; to move to a previous cell press Shift-Tab. You can always position the cursor with the mouse anywhere in the table cells. You may want to make some of the following changes to the information in your table.

- **Changing the size of the table**: Position the cursor anywhere in a table cell, select Table, Insert (or Delete), type in the number of columns or rows to add (or delete), and select OK. You can also add rows by clicking in the last column, and clicking Tab for as many cells as you want to add. You can delete columns or rows by selecting them and pressing Delete (but select Table, Delete... in Word. Also be sure that the cells have handles on them.)

- **Changing the width of a column**: Position the cursor on the column line you want to change, and when you see the width change cursor, drag the line left or right to the size you want.

- **Changing the appearance, size, or justification of text in your columns or rows**: Highlight the columns or rows you want to change, select the appropriate button and make the changes.

- **Changing the lines or fill in your table**: Highlight the rows, columns, or cells you want to change the lines or fill on, select Lines from the Table Tool Bar, and select the desired lines or fill.

With these functions, you should be able to create an interesting, easy to read table of complex information.

Columns

If you want to do a newsletter or brochure for an organization you belong to, you may want to be able to use multiple columns in your documents rather than the standard one column of text. WP can help you achieve interesting effects with its Column feature. To use columns, select Columns on the Tool bar and indicate how many columns you want.

There are two basic types of columns: newspaper and parallel. **Newspaper** columns move from top to bottom of the left column to top to bottom of the right, to top to bottom of the left on the next page, etc. **Parallel** columns are independent of each other. What you put in the left column continues to the top of the left column of the next page, not to the top of the right column on the same page. Usually, you will use newspaper columns, unless you have information in the left column that needs to be opposite specific information in the right column.

You can change the appearance of your columns by selecting Format, Columns. Here you can make additional changes to your columns. See Help for additional information about using, navigating in, and discontinuing columns.

With the addition of graphics, tables, and columns, WP functions nearly as well as many desktop publishing programs. You will be able to add interesting effects to your word processed documents, effects that can reinforce your message and help your readers to understand it.

Lesson 9 — Advanced Features

WP includes many more features than have been discussed so far. Some of them are meant for specific professions, such as the legal profession which has specific needs in documents. Others are for writers who create complex documents with mathematical formulas, tables, charts, and graphics. With practice, using most of these options is actually not too complex. Because they are beyond what most students need to use, here we have simply suggested the range of possibilities using features that experienced users rely on to simplify their work.

Experienced users simplify their word processing tasks whenever they can. Although some of the WP time savers presented in this lesson take a little time to learn, in the long run they will shorten the time you will need to spend at the computer.

Date

One time saver is the date function. WP reproduces the date upon command. Using Insert, Date and Time, places the current date at the cursor. You can select the format of the date, 6/25/2001 or 25 June 2001, for example. If you retrieve the document with the Date in it a day, a week, a month, or even a year later, WP will put in the date you inserted. If you'd rather have the date change to the current date each time you open the document, use Insert, Date and Time, and tell WP to update the date to keep it current.

Macro

Another time saver is the macro function. A macro is a series of frequently used characters or keystrokes which can be "replayed" from the Tools menu simply by selecting Macro, Play. For example, every time you want to create a header or footer, you need to select Insert (or View), Headers and Footers, type in text, change fonts, styles, sizes, margins, etc. Instead of having to type these keystrokes and wait each time you need them, you can create a macro and then "play" it to carry out all the necessary steps automatically.

Creating a Macro

Any series of keystrokes, commands, or text may be created or "recorded" in a macro. WP performs each item in exactly the same order as you created it. To create and record a macro select Tools, Macro, Record. A dialog box appears in which you name the macro you are creating. Since this is the name you will use each time you use or "play" this macro, make the name something short that you can easily remember and type. Name the macro with a name of 1 - 8 characters long. You can also assign keystrokes to a macro or put the marco on a Tool bar. After typing a name for your named macro, select Record.

In Record mode type the exact text, mouse selections, keystrokes, or commands you want in your macro. You can use any of the menu selections, regular, special or function keys, format commands (such as changes of tabs, margin settings, line spacing), or other keystrokes that will produce the desired macro. Unfortunately, all of your typing mistakes and corrections will also be recorded. Accurate typing makes the macro play faster by eliminating extra steps. When you have completed typing the characters and commands for your macro, select Stop. You can then play the macro by selecting Tools, Macro, Play, pressing the keyboard shortcut you assigned to the macro, or selecting the macro from the Tool bar.

Playing a Macro

You can play a macro by selecting Tools, Macro, Macro (or Play), pressing the keyboard shortcut you assigned to the macro, or selecting the macro from the Tool bar. WP automatically inserts the text from the macro or performs the tasks designated in the macro.

Find/Replace

Even careful typists make mistakes in typing text. For example, you may have misspelled an author's name throughout an essay focused on her midwestern fiction. Since WP's spell check will probably not have the correct spelling of her name in its dictionary, you may not have corrected her name while you ran spell check. After realizing the correct spelling, you can spell check the whole document again, or use a real time saver Find and Replace.

You can search for any combination of letters, words, phrases, clauses, keystrokes, or codes from the cursor position forward or backward. In each case, the procedure is the same.

After selecting Edit, Find (or Find and Replace), in the dialog box type the word or phrase you want to find. Do not press Enter unless the word you seek is followed by a hard return. Using the mouse, move the cursor to the Replace With: box or tab and type in the correct spelling or codes you need to use. Next, locate the cursor at the position in your document where you want the search to begin.

Be certain you relocate the cursor in the text if you have used the scroll bar. If your cursor in not in the right position, the search may fail to locate the word you are looking for.

You may select one of two search options in the dialog box. If you select Find Next, WP will find the next instance of the object of your search and highlight it. You can then click Replace to correct that instance. Or, with the cursor in position at the start of the document, you can select Replace All in the dialog box and WP will find and correct all the designated erroneous words or codes you specified.

If you told WP to search for *prompt* and automatically replace each instance with *message*, you will find such things as *prompts* changed to *messages*, and *prompting* to *messageing*. To prevent the computer from automatically changing each instance of *prompt* including *impromptu* to *immessageu*, you may have to type *prompt* with spaces before and after the word to make sure that only *prompt* is replaced with *message*. After using find and replace, you will find that it is easy to use and saves many minutes of visually searching your document.

Find Files

Occasionally you will forget where you stored information that you need for a paper. This happens because many filenames are not as descriptive as they could be and because, while working on a project, you will collect a large number of files related to your topic. Windows Explorer and WP both provide help with finding files and information on a particular topic.

Click Search in Windows Explorer to search for a file with a specific phrase or word in it. Indicate the folder that you want to search, and then click Search Now.

Windows Explorer displays a thumbnail of the file you have selected. WP will also display a preview of the selected document when you select File, Open, and make sure that Views, Preview (or Toggle Preview On/Off) is selected.

Probably the best way to locate files you need for your research project is to keep all your files in sensible folders so that you can readily locate what you need and not spend useless time searching for lost items. Whenever you open or save a file, be sure to note the disk drive, folder, and subfolder of the file.

Save As

When you save files, you may occasionally want to save them in another format, such as ASCII (DOS text), HTML, RTF (Rich Text Format), Word, or WordPerfect. This enables you to work with the files on another computer that does not have WP. If WP does not have any of the formats your computer can read, you can always save the file as an ASCII text, which nearly every word processing program can read. However, you will lose all the formatting if you use this option. ASCII (DOS text) is often useful, however, for preparing e-mail messages "off line" because many mail programs cannot use WP files.

Select File, Save As, and select the format you want to save your document to. WP automatically adds the correct extension, txt, htm, rtf, doc, or wpd to your filename.

You can also open files saved in different formats. When you attempt to open an ASCII file, for example, WP will give you a dialog box with its best guess on the non-WP file format. If WP has correctly identified the file type, select OK. If it has not, select the Convert File Format From button, and scroll through the selections until you find the right one. Select the file format and then OK. This automatic conversion of ASCII, ANSI, and various word processing file types is useful when you are working on various types of computers and with other people who may not have the same hardware and software as you. This same feature also makes it possible to share files with Macintosh users if the files are saved and converted properly on the Macintosh before you put the disk in a Windows machine.

Templates

All WP documents are actually based on a template. All of the documents you have created so far are based on a "standard" template that is automatically loaded each time you load WP. WP also includes a set of predesigned templates to simplify creating different types of documents such as calendars, memos, newsletters, resumes, and other types of documents.

Many of these templates use an "autofill" function that allows you to enter information such as your name, address, phone number, and company name only once and then reuse it each time you use a specific template.

To use a template other than the default one, select File, New (or New from Project). A dialog box displays a list of choices.

Perhaps the most useful template for students in the resume wizard. You can select a variety of different formats for your resume. When you have selected a specific type for the first time, such as Professional, WP begins the autofill process. You will be asked for your name, address, date, etc. WP then puts the cursor in the first preset section of the resume where you can fill in your objective, experience, education, and skills. Then save the file normally so that you can print it or revise it when applying for a different job.

Lesson 9 - Advanced Features

Although the formats suggested by some of the templates are not necessarily exciting or spectacular as graphic designs, they have the advantage of suggesting a beginning format, content, and graphics pattern that is consistent with professional document production. If you have no idea where to start with your resume or a newsletter, they do provide a very useful starting point.

Most templates incorporate various paragraph styles; that is, the paragraph has been designed with a default font face and size, space above and below, tab settings, indents, and other text formatting features. Thus, rather than resetting all these settings when you want to use a bulleted hanging indented list, simply select Format, Styles, select List: All styles, and select the appropriate style such as List Bullet to apply to your paragraph. You can create and modify styles to suit your particular needs. Using styles throughout your documents helps create consistency in format and saves considerable time in formatting various text styles.

Downloading Software

The Internet provides a vast resource for inexpensive or free software. The most common need for special software is to view files, graphics, or listen to music found on the WWW. Most browsers tell you if you try to open or download a file which requires a special program you don't have to access the file. Many of the electronic databases may also require special programs to print full-text articles properly. In both of these cases you may be automatically taken to a site where the proper program is available.

Many web sites offer downloadable programs. You can find some of the most common programs such as Mulberry and WS-FTP at the UMD Information Technology pages. Other sites providing vast collections of software are tucows.com, shareware,com, and Stroud's Consummate WinApps at cws.internet.com/.

Unfortunately, most of the downloaded programs need to be installed before they will run. Also, many of the files are "compressed" or "zipped" to make them download faster. You may have to download a program such as WinZip before you can install the program you are really interested in running.

With these advanced features of WP, you can perform complicated, time-consuming tasks with ease. You will also have the flexibility to work with various file formats and locate software on the Internet. Using macros, Find/ Replace, and templates will help you spend less time at the computer and more time doing other things.

Computing for College Writing

Lesson 10 — Shortcuts

Having used WP for some time now, you should have a fairly good feel for the features most commonly used in word processing. Although WP has many other special application features such as styles, outline and index generator, sort/merge, we have covered the features most applicable to composition. As you continue to use the computer in your writing, you may find that some of the shortcuts listed below will help you in your future word processing at the University.

Printing a Block

Occasionally, you may want to print only a portion of a page of text, particularly when you are revising an essay. To do this, highlight the text you want to print, select File, Print. In the Print dialog box, make sure that Selected text (or Selection) is marked; select Print. Only the selected text will print.

Note that if you select the Print button on the Tool bar in Word, you do not get a chance to print only the selected text. The entire document will print.

Printing Multiple Pages

If you are doing a revision of an essay and have made substantial changes only on pages 3 to 6, you might want to print only those pages. To do this, select File, Print. In the dialog box ndicate the pages you want to print in Pages (or Multiple pages or Print pages). Type in the page numbers you want to print, 3-6 in the above example, or 7,9,12 and select Print. Just pages 3 to 6 and 7, 9, and 12 will print.

Quick Highlighting

When blocking text you may have found that the arrow keys are a slow method of highlighting text particularly on some older machines. You can mark blocks of text with the mouse by clicking on the position where you want to begin marking the block, holding down the left mouse button, and dragging the mouse cursor over the desired text. Or you can double click to select one word, triple click to select one sentence (or one paragraph in Word), and quadruple click for a paragraph in WordPerfect.

If you want to select the entire document, select Edit, Select All or press Ctrl-a. The entire document will be highlighted.

Combining Documents

You may have occasion to put one document at the end of another or at a specific position other than at the end. You may be revising an essay for which you have the introduction in one document, the body in a second, and the conclusion in a third document. To put these together can be easily done in WP.

Open one of the files you want combined. Position the cursor where you want the new file to be added. Without exiting the document, select

Insert, File. Double click the file you want inserted into the first document. You will now have the first document with the second document added at the cursor location. Be sure to save the new document with the File, Save As command to give it a new name.

Managing Files

Probably the most frustrating problem is to lose information through computer or power malfunction (or user abuse). Always make sure you have current backup copies of your important documents. SAVE your work often! Use the Save As command to save with a different name. Renaming files allows you to keep copies of earlier editions of a text or to create a copy of the text with a new name. If you have copies, you can often recover the file even if the disk is damaged or if you accidentally make a major change you did not intend.

One handy feature of the Open dialog boxes is the set of menu items and the buttons on and below the Menu Bar (see the graphic below). Open File allows you to delete, rename, or copy files and create shortcuts. You can select the drive, directory, subdirectory, and filename in the dialog box and then right click to perform any of these file management tasks. Buttons on the Toolbar perform such functions as cut, copy, paste, delete, and changing icons. Notice the difference between WordPerfect's Open File and Word's Open dialog boxes pictured on the next page.

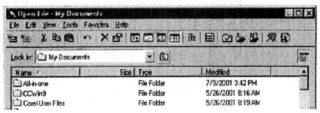

WordPerfect's Open File Dialog Box

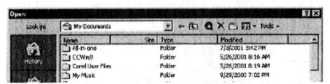

Word's Open Dialog Box

Another useful feature of the Open dialog box is the Preview function. If you are uncertain what is in a certain file, simply select the file and select Views, Preview (or select the Toggle Preview On/Off button on the Tool bar). Preview opens a Viewer window with a small image of the text of the selected document. You can scroll through the document to see if it indeed is the file you want to open.

Another feature that can be turned on is the file selection choices at the bottom of the File Menu option. Here you may see a list of four to ten files; these are the last files opened in WP. If you are using a stand alone computer (your personal computer, for example) with most of your work stored on the hard disk, you can select any of these files to open. Thus if you worked on a document but remembered something you should have included in it while you are working on another, you can save the current document, select File, Open, click the previous document, and make the changes. This feature may not work on networked computers.

To prevent problems, examine your disks periodically to delete or archive to backup disks unused or unneeded documents. When the number of documents on your disk approaches 100, use another disk. When your directory shows only 100,000 bytes free on your disk, use another disk. With too many files or too little space left on a disk, information becomes very vulnerable to destruction.

Using Multiple Windows

WP functions just as other Windows programs function; they all use the Windows feature. You can minimize a WP document. Your document and the WP program become a small icon in the Taskbar at the bottom of the screen, and you will be returned usually to the desktop or another window depending on how your computer has been set up. You now can run another software program such as a graphics or spreadsheet program or run applications such as email. Windows allows you to copy and paste from various programs to WP. If your information is in a mail message, this is an easy way to get it into a WP document. Note that text you copy and paste from WP to some email programs may lose all the WP formatting. When you want to return to WP, either minimize or exit the application you were working on and click the WP minimized icon. You will return to your document.

You can also open multiple documents. Each document you open goes into a window on top of any other windows you currently have open. Thus if you are revising an essay you might want to open a new file, save it as a new filename, and then open the old version of the essay. This way you can copy and paste from one document to another. To switch from one document to another select Window. You will see all the open documents listed at the bottom of the menu with a check mark by the document you are currently using. Select the document you want to go to, and WP brings that document to the top, putting the document you were using on the bottom. Thus, you can toggle from one document to another, as needed.

Using Macros and Fields

WordPerfect has several preinstalled macros that you might find useful. For example, if you want to keep track of the filename of your document by placing it in a footer, you can use the filestmp macro to place the document filename automatically at the cursor position. Any of the macros in the macro directory may be used in your documents. If you are uncertain what the individual macro does, search WordPerfect's Help for Macro, then supplied with WordPerfect to view the list of macros.

To insert the filename of your document in a footer in Word, however, select Insert, Field, Document Information, FileName. Word inserts the filename in uppercase. To change the filename to lowercase, click Options, in Formatting

select Lowercase, click Add to Field, and click
OK.

Using Endnotes or Footnotes

When doing research papers, writers often com-
plain of the time-consuming task of arranging
footnotes at the bottom of the page or putting
endnotes at the end of the paper. WP handles
both of these tasks effortlessly, including keeping track of the numbering, so that if you delete
one note, the rest of the notes are automatically
renumbered throughout the text. Both types of
notes are an Insert function; select the type you
want, create the note, and off you go to a finished research paper.

Using Symbols

Often you will need to use a special character in
your document: for example, ¶ , ™, or $. Of
course, if the character is not on the keyboard,
you could leave some space in your document
and then pencil the character in after you print
the document. In many cases, this will not be
necessary, especially if the character you need
is one of the symbols in WP. Select Insert, Symbol. You will see a dialog box with a Set selector
(or a Font and Subset selector) and a character
view box. Select one of the different sets available, select the character you want, and select
Insert to put the character in your document.
You may have to hunt for the symbol you want;
Word has the trademark and copyright symbols
in Special Characters, whereas WordPerfect
puts these symbols in a Typographic character
set. Look around for what you need. Now you

can have many different characters in your documents; you will be freed forever from the penciled-in character.

Tool Bars

As with most everything in WP, the Tool bars are changeable and can be customized to suit your needs and desires. The one that automatically appears when you open WP is the default tool bar. To select a different Tool bar simply place the mouse over the Tool bar and click the right mouse button. A list of Tool bars appears. Select the one you want with the mouse, and it is added to the existing Toolbar. You can shorten the time you spend at the computer if you have the appropriate Tool bars opened that you will use frequently while working on your document. If you are working on a web page, for example, you might want to turn on the Web Tool Bar or the Hypertext Tool Bar.

Using Help

Occasionally you will forget how to perform a word processing function, mail merge, for example. You can use Help to find answers to your questions. Select Help, then select Ask the PerfectExpert or Show the Office Assistant (also known as Clipit, the paper clip that appears on your Word document). You can also search the Help index by selecting Help, Microsoft Word Help or Help Topics. Everything you wanted to know but were afraid to ask is located in Help.

As you use WP, you will find other shortcut methods to make your word processing tasks

easier. Practice using the WP commands to perform more and more complicated word processing tasks; manage your documents effectively
by using utility commands; take care of your
original and backup disks. You will wonder how
you ever survived without a computer and word
processing.

Computing for College Writing

Name _____

Section _____

1. What is the difference between endnotes and footnotes?

2. How do you display the symbols your WP program has? Indicate which WP program you are using.

3. How can you tell how many windows you have open?

4. How do you automatically put the filename in your footer? Indicate which WP program you are using.

5. How do you change the Tool bar?

6. Give the steps for printing only pages one, three, and five of a ten page document.

7. What are the options you can perform from the Open (File) dialog box? Indicate which WP program you are using.

8. Give the steps for copying a paragraph from document 1 to document 2.

9. Give the steps for viewing a file without actually opening it. Indicate which WP program you are using.

10. Give the steps for quickly highlighting this sentence; use the fewest actions possible. Indicate which WP program you are using.

The Appearance of Printed Texts

Until electronic equipment for producing printed texts in a single copy or two became widely available, the best text that an individual could produce probably came from a typewriter. A lucky few used electric or electronic typewriters to produce texts in a few different type faces, usually Pica or Elite, Letter Gothic or some cross between script and Italic. `Most of their texts—letters and reports, legal briefs and contracts, memos and drafts ready for publication—looked something like this section of the paragraph.` Such texts were rarely attractive, but nobody expected elegance except in the products of a printing press. This expectation, alas, still drives the styles advocated in numerous style manuals.

In a course that requires your writing a paper almost every week, you do not have time to create beautifully-designed texts for every draft that your produce. But you do you should produce texts that are at least pleasant to look at and physically easy to read. Without resorting to the complexities of desktop publishing, you can produce attractive, readable drafts. Most good word processing programs provide full control over the features that most contribute to the appearance and readability of a printed text. Here are some features of format and page design that you should keep in mind as you produce your final drafts for this course as well as for the other courses that you take at UMD.

- *Top and Bottom Margins:* Balance your text between top and bottom margins. Use wide enough margins to provide a frame for each page. The WordPerfect default setting is 1", which is safe but not especially attractive or economical when using headers. (See suggestions for using and for placing headers below.) You may also have to adjust the alignment of the paper in a printer.

- *Right and Left Margins:* Follow same general principle as that outlined above. Remember to allow for **binding offset** when you use covers or another kind of binder (rare in this course). Do not be afraid to increase or decrease margins to suit your text.

- *Choice of Font:* Choose a base font that is readable and preferably attractive as well. Even the simplest printer will give you choice of fonts, along with some common variants as italics, underlining, boldfacing. Better quality printers usually provide a variety of fonts, some of which are scalable (allowing for minute variations in size). The base font of this appendix is 10 point Verdana. As you will see, we can easily vary the fonts many times within this brief text, and not always with pleasant results.

- *Title:* Provide a title that gives a clear sense of the subject of your paper or focuses on an important theme in it. Don't leave your readers guessing.

- *Widows and Orphans:* It is an act of insensitivity if not cruelty to create either widows or orphans in printed texts. Not only do widows and orphans distort relationships in blocks of text. They also make trouble for readers trying to understand blocks of text that should stay together. A widow—the bereaved mother without her family—sits alone at the bottom of a page. An orphan, in contrast, is a lonely survivor separated from its family, sitting alone at the top of the next page. Word processors can automatically avoid such violations of the family. Conditional page commands take care of the problem. In WordPerfect just select Format, Keep Text Together options; in Word select Format, Paragraph, and then select the Line and Page Breaks tab. Giving WP widow/orphan commands will eliminate widows and orphans in your document.

- *Headers and Footers:* A header is a running line of information at the top of a printed page. Headers usually identify the subject of the text on the page. They often give chapter titles, for example. They often provide page numbers as well—usually at the left and right sides of pages in an open book. Take at look at the header on the top line of type on this page. It identifies the subject of the text. The footer identifies the book tiele and the current page. The proper command in a header or footer automatically paginates the text once you enter the command. To enter a header in WordPerfect select Insert, Header/Footer (in Word, select View, Header and Footer). Then follow the instructions on the drop-down menu. To enter page numbers, select Insert, Page Numbers or click the Insert Page Number button on the Header and Footer Tool Bar in Word (in

WordPerfect, select Format, Page, Insert Page Number).

- *Placing Headers on a Page:* The default top margin in WordPerfect (1") wastes space on a printed page and throws the page layout badly out of balance when using headers. (Word's default top margin setting is 0.5"—a setting that places headers where they belong.) The solution when using WordPerfect is to reduce the top margin to 0.3" or 0.4"; then enter the header, ending it by pressing ENTER. This will place the header within the top margin and begin the text below it, leaving a decent amount of space between the header and the first line of text. A good practice is to change the header from that of the first page to subsequent ones. Give the full information usually asked for on class assignments on the first page. On subsequent pages, reduce the header to a single line with a short title. Include in it its subject and the page number.

  A header entered anywhere after the top of a file will supersede the first one. Changing headers is therefore very easy in most word processing programs.

- *Page Numbering:* Essays and papers, reports and editorials, memos and instructions, proposals and directives, novels and reviews should all have page numbers (pieces of paper, especially stapled or loose sheets, can get mixed up). You can place them in headers or footers or use the WP's command or menu. Avoid bottom or top centered page numbers. They look like manuscript rather than book or periodical format.

- *Block Indentation:* Sometimes these are called "Block Indents." Use Block Indentation to separate included blocks of text from your main text. The indentation from the left is essential. You may also, if you choose, indent at the same time from the right margin. In published books and periodicals you will frequently see a change in the font as well. The entries behind the bullet headers are all block indents. So is this one:

  For this block of text I have indented 1 tab stop from the left margin, but the right margin remains at the default. By now you probably have noticed that the font has also changed—to 9 point Arial Rounded MT, a blocky-looking font without serifs ("sans serif"), the short ornamental lines that terminate the main horizontal, vertical, and curved lines of characters with serifs (like Times Roman). The font returns to 10 point Verdana in the next entry.

- *Tab Settings:* Most word processing programs set default tabs to .5" intervals. For letters, memos, and drafts of papers, these will suit most needs. But sometimes you must change these settings to create an effective display or to improve the appearance of a page. The first Tab setting for this file, for example, is at 0.25"—which reduces an otherwise large gap between the blocked text and the bullet headers. If you want to put data in columns you can simplify the job by eliminating all tab settings but those that you need.

Appendix 1 - The Appearance of Printed Texts

- *Justification:* Justification is simply the alignment of a text—to the left, to the right, to the left and right ("full"), to the center, or to a specific position within the text. Left justification is so common in written and printed texts that we often ignore its use. This text is both left justified above, and it looks satisfactory because its characters are proportionally spaced. But in this block I have changed to a fixed-pitch font, resulting in unsightly gaps and channels. When using a fixed-pitch font, such as Courier 10, turn off the right justification (use left justification only).

- *Hyphenation:* Splitting words between syllables at the end of a line is called "hyphenation." As the term implies, a hyphen marks the point of division. Hyphenation can save space, and it can improve the appearance of texts printed in fixed-pitch fonts. Any good word processor can provide automatic hyphenation. But don't turn it on until you format your final draft. It can interfere with efficient editing.

- *Heading and Subtitles:* The use of headings, subtitles, and symbols such as bullet headers can improve the readability of long texts. Indeed, their use is expected in many kinds of discourse (e.g., proposals, reports, sets of directions). Bullets and numbers are always placed to the left of the verbal text. Headings and subtitles may be left justified or centered. Their placement usually depends upon the way that information is classified. For example, major sections may be marked with centered headings and subsections with left-justified headings.

These features by no means exhaust the resources available to you in most full-featured word processing programs. The capacity to incorporate graphics with verbal text character- izes most current, mainline programs allows you to create both intellectually interesting and visually pleasing documents.

They permit easy insertion of boxes for text, tables, and graphics; they permit the insertion of verti- cal or horizontal lines to set off text or graphics anywhere on a page. They support a variety of multiple- column formats. Most lines can be infinitely varied in size and shading, and most programs even sup- port free-form draw- ing if desired.

These two short col- umns are in a simple newspaper format with a quarter-inch space between them. The vertical line may be inserted without any further modifica- tions of the layout. And notice also that columns may be turned on and off at will as easily as the style and point size of a font may be changed.

The columns above have been turned off to permit insertion of a line between the text above and this new paragraph. The format allows the insertion of an illustration from Vol. 1 of an eighteenth-century edition of Joseph Addison's *Miscellaneous Works* (1765).

Frontispiece to Joseph Addison, *The Miscellaneous Works in Verse and Prose*. Ed. Thomas Tickell. 4 vols. London: J. and R. Tonson, 1765). Reprinted with permission from the library of W. A. Gibson.

Style Manuals in College Writing

Anyone who compares the style used in the two manuals for College Writing course with that advocated by *The MLA Style Manual* (or the *Publication Manual of the American Psychological Association*, the "APA") will immediately notice a few significant differences. For example, we italicize the titles of books and periodicals; we do not underline them, and we certainly do not underline punctuation marks. Information set off in Block Indents is single-spaced, not double; block indents are separated from the text that precedes and follows them with double rather than triple spacing, and they are indented a single tab stop from the left margin (not 1"). **Works Cited** citations have hanging indents and they are single- rather than double-spaced. These discrepancies are easily explained, and they are, in fact, consistent with the conventions of the style manuals.

The differences are implicit in the titles of the manuals, for example, *MLA Handbook for Writers of Research Papers*. The conventions listed above are all conventions used for preparing papers (manuscripts) for publication. They are conventions used more by copy-editors and typesetters rather than by readers. They are intended to reduce the likelihood of errors when preparing a manuscript for publication. A copy-editor and typesetter know that a <u>single underline</u> represents *italic type*, a <u>double underline</u> represents SMALL CAPS, a wavy line represents **boldface**, and a triple underline represents UPPER-CASE CAPS. The extra spacing around and within Block Indents is intended to distinguish the blocked text from the body text and to leave room for copy-editing. Manuscripts prepared on most typewriters provide no other way to make distinctions that printed texts and word-processed texts can more economically and intuitively represent.

The distinctions between manuscripts and printed texts are clear when one reads the style manuals carefully. For example, the APA *Publications Manual* gives the following instruction and explanation:

> In a manuscript for publication, **all references are to be double-spaced and indented**. Just as a double-spaced manuscript page is typeset as a single-spaced page, the paragraph indent in a reference entry will be converted to a hanging indent when typeset. (4th ed., 1994. 194)

The conventions in the APA manual have a single purpose: to produce typescripts that will eventually be printed and published. Furthermore, this passage suggests that somehow the format and style will automatically be corrected when manuscripts are set in type for publication. They will not be corrected **automatically** or reformatted without the intervention of human editors and probably computerized typesetters as well. Readers, in contrast, have come to expect a different set of conventions—ones that reflect the conventions and editorial practices of written texts that they routinely see in print.

Most writers today think more of readers' expectations than those of copy-editors'. They write term papers and memos, grant proposals and letters, advertisements and sets of instructions for readers. Increasingly writers use word-processing programs to emulate printed texts even for distribution within and institution, agency, or corporation. They take for granted the need on many occasions to produce camera-ready copy for publication. The electronic file produced by a word-processing program often creates a plate for printing without the intervention of a copy-editor laboriously marking up a text produced on a typewriter. The conventions in our manuals recognize and teach practices used in most businesses and institutions worldwide. We see no point in using modern technology to emulate a manual typewriter.

The simplest explanation for the conventions illustrated in the College Writing manuals is that we show what the MLA conventions **represent** when they govern the style of a finished text rather than the conventions of a working draft or copy text. They enable students to produce texts that are reasonably attractive, consistent with the MLA style, readable, and economical.

 We take such a position confident that most of our students will enter professions in which they will routinely be expected to produce high quality texts rather than typescripts for copy-editors.